Bonsai

4451
©1995 Coombe Books
This edition published in 1995 by Coombe Books
for Parragon Book Service Ltd, Unit 13-17
Avonbridge Trading Estate, Atlantic Road,
Avonbridge, Bristol BS11 9QD
Printed in Hong Kong
ISBN 1-85813-8396

Bonsai

Text by
COLIN LEWIS
Photography by
NEIL SUTHERLAND

||| •PARRAGON• |||

Contents

Introduction
Pages 6-13

Growing
Pages 14-37

Creating Styles
Pages 38-59

Special Projects
Pages 60-73

Care
Pages 74-93

Glossary
Pages 94-96

Acknowledgments
Page 96

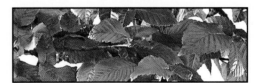

Introduction

The two syllables of the Japanese word bonsai literally translate as 'a tree in a pot', but when combined they acquire an altogether grander meaning. A bonsai is a plant which is established in an aesthetically harmonious container, and has been subjected to a number of horticultural and sculptural techniques in order to create a tree-like image. At one end of the spectrum these images are virtually exact replicas of their full-sized cousins. At the other end they can become abstract sculptures, inspired by the landscapes of the mind.

A bonsai is not a naturally dwarfed variety, neither is it treated with any special potion to stop it growing larger. Its growth is not restricted by confining the roots in a pot, but by constant clipping and trimming.

▲ A commercial bonsai farm near Takamatsu, Japan.

How old is a bonsai?

A bonsai does not have to be old to be good. It is quite possible to create a delightful little tree in an afternoon, as you will see later in this book, although until it is established in its pot it is not a true bonsai. Having said this, bonsai do improve with age. Bark texture, trunk taper, branch structure, fine twigs and so on require time to develop, even with a helping hand. So over the years, with the right care and attention, a good bonsai can become a better bonsai. However, a poorly designed young tree can only become a poorly designed old tree, so it is essential to get the basic form right from the start.

Origins

No-one knows exactly when the first bonsai was grown, but we do know that the ancient Chinese cultivated miniature landscapes in shallow containers. Complete with trees, rocks and mosses, these landscapes, or penjing, were the forerunners of bonsai. The first pictorial records of penjing appeared in Chinese temple murals during the Han dynasty, around 200BC.

Single tree plantings came later, but exactly when is unclear. These were called pun-sai, the Chinese root of the Japanese word bonsai. In fact the Japanese and Chinese characters for the two terms are identical. When the Chinese invaded Japan in the Middle Ages they introduced, amongst other things, the Buddhist religion. The monks at that time were custodians of all forms of cultural heritage and took with them their written language, their art and their bonsai. For centuries the ownership

世 界 盆 栽 大 会 記 念
'89 WORLD BONSAI CONVENTION

POST OFFICE

◀ A first day cover produced in commemoration of the World Bonasi Convention, held in Omiya, Japan 1989.

of bonsai was restricted to those of noble birth or high office. At that time all bonsai were created from ancient stunted trees collected from the mountains, where their constant battle with the harsh environment had restricted their size and given them gnarled and twisted shapes. The tenacity of these trees was held in such reverence that they were deemed to possess spiritual qualities which would be inherited by their owners.

It was not until this century that the ordinary citizen began to practice bonsai, by which time it had become a highly refined and structured discipline. Such was the commitment of the dedicated bonsai artist that a group of them decided to further their art by forming the "bonsai village', Omiya, which is now an outer suburb of Tokyo and a mecca for bonsai enthusiasts the world over.

Bonsai in the West

The Second World War was responsible for the spread of bonsai to the West. British and American troops returning from the far east brought memories, pictures and some live examples of these curious little trees. Few knew what they were or how to care for them, but in spite of this there are still a few of these original imports alive today.

As the awareness gradually spread, so did the thirst for more knowledge. A few western enthusiasts visited Japan to learn more and returned to spread the word. By the late sixties small commercial nurseries were in business, importing a few hundred trees a year. Nowadays bonsai is a household word and hundreds of thousands of plants are imported annually, although not all from Japan. These are tropical species which do not tolerate our climate and must be kept indoors for much of the year. Trees do not grow well under these conditions. They prefer to be exposed to the sun, wind and rain, where their seasonal changes can be fully appreciated.

The future

It is the responsibility of each dedicated bonsai enthusiast to develop the art further by applying the techniques to local species, creating new styles in the process. Therefore, in this book we concentrate entirely on familiar species which will happily thrive outdoors all year round with very little extra winter protection. But there is only so much you can learn from the printed page. Practical experience is the best teacher.

◀ This bonsai is quite large at 22in tall. It was collected only six years ago from a roadside verge, and was planted directly into a bonsai container.

◀ This medium sized bonsai stands 11in tall from the rim of the pot. It was collected 11 years ago.

Size and age

One of the first questions people ask on their initial encounter with bonsai is, 'How old is it?' They are naturally fascinated by these ancient-looking specimens, and the thought that they have been cared for by successive generations of devoted artists. In many cases, especially with collected wild trees, it is impossible to know the exact age, one can only guess. As one bonsai master says: 'You should never ask a beautiful woman her age'.

Once you have grown a few bonsai yourself, you will realise just how unimportant the true age really is compared with the apparent age. More significant is the length of time the tree has been in training as a bonsai. Even this is of secondary importance when compared to the beauty of form, colour and texture of a lovely bonsai, whatever its age.

Size is another factor whose importance is frequently over-rated. It is often assumed that the larger the bonsai, the older, and therefore the better it is. This is not true. It is also often assumed that bigger bonsai are technically and aesthetically more difficult to create. Also not true.

In fact a small or shohin bonsai requires more ingenuity and patience to create, because the artist has to work with fewer elements, yet still has to aspire to the same aesthetic standards which apply to very much larger trees.

A shohin bonsai also demands far more constant attention to maintain than many of the other types. The pots dry out far quicker than other bonsais, shoots outgrow the design more often and, if the bonsai is left to grow for too long, will sap the energy from the fine twigs, causing them to wither and die.

Your bonsai is the result of an interaction between you and nature, and the success of everything you do relies upon the tree's natural response to your actions. In order to get the best out of your hobby it is important to have at least a basic understanding of how a tree works.

Roots

Roots have three functions. One, quite simply, is to hold the tree steady in the soil. This is performed by thick, strong roots which radiate from the base of the trunk. Evidence which came to light after the great storm in 1987 in the UK suggests that these roots only penetrate the soil a few feet, and the existence of an extensive tap root was only a myth.

The second function is to store nutrients during the dormant period, ready for use when growth resumes in spring.

The third function is to absorb water and nutrients, via tiny, single-cell protrusions called root hairs, which clothe the young roots as they grow.

Root problems

Apart from insect attack the only serious problem you will need to cope with is root rot, which is easier to prevent than cure. Decay is caused by microscopic fungi or bacteria which take hold on dead roots, so the simple answer is to ensure that the roots remain healthy at all times.

The first precaution is to use a free-draining soil with plenty of air spaces. This prevents the roots 'drowning' and is inhospitable to unwanted fungi. Similarly, you should never allow the soil to dry out, as this will also kill young, tender roots, exposing them to decay.

The second precaution is to avoid over-feeding. Roots absorb water by osmosis, whereby a weak solution passes through a membrane (the wall of the root) towards a stronger solution. If the water in the soil contains a stronger solution of nutrients than that in the root, water will pass from the root back into the soil depriving the tree of water.

The first signs of root rot are yellowing or wilting of the leaves, die-back of young shoots, or a sudden lack of vigour. Your first reaction is likely to be to increase the feed and water, either of which will compound the problem.

The trunk and branches

Like roots, the trunk and branches also perform three functions. The first is structural, supporting the branches and foliage. The second, also like roots, is to store nutrients until needed. This is done in specially adapted cells which radiate from the centre of the trunk in bundles called medullary rays. The third function is to carry water and nutrients from one part of the tree to another. This takes place towards the outer edge of the trunk, either side of the cambium layer.

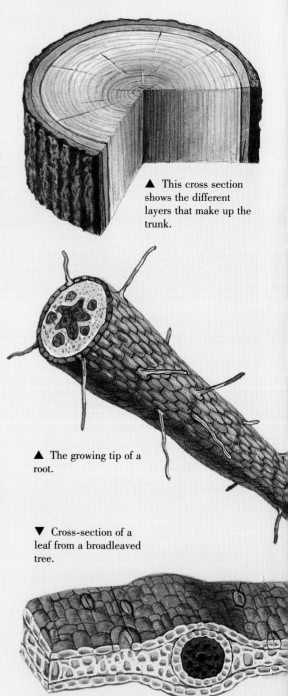

▲ This cross section shows the different layers that make up the trunk.

▲ The growing tip of a root.

▼ Cross-section of a leaf from a broadleaved tree.

◀ This gorgeous azalea (rhododendron indicum) is kept in vibrant health by its owner. The bi-coloured flowers make this variety so desirable.

The cambium layer

This is really the 'magic' part of the tree, responsible for controlling the growth. It is a single-cell layer just beneath the bark and appears green when the bark is scraped away in most species (in some conifers it is orange or yellow). During the growing season the cambium layer produces a new layer of tissue on either side. On the inside is the sapwood, or xylem, through which the water is transported from the roots throughout the tree. Each season this xylem is replaced by a new layer, creating the familiar growth rings. On the outside the new layer is called the phloem, and this is responsible for distributing the sugars produced in the leaves to other parts of the tree. This, too, is replaced each year and the build-up of old phloem layers forms the thick, corky bark we see on older trees.

The cambium layer is also responsible for producing new roots in cuttings and air layers, and adventitious buds, as well as the tissue which heals over wounds. When grafting, the cambium layers of the two components fuse together, enabling them to operate as one plant.

Foliage

All leaves are basically food factories, using light as a catalyst to convert water supplied by the roots and carbon dioxide absorbed from the air into sugars, in a process called photosynthesis. These sugars provide growth energy to the plant. During the day the leaves 'breathe in' through small pores called stomata, and at night they expel the excess oxygen and other gaseous by-products. They also allow water to evaporate through the surface in order to keep up a constant flow. Some leaves, particularly the needles of pines and spruces, have waxy coating to help conserve moisture during the winter, when the roots are frozen and unable to function. This coating also serves to prevent snow and ice adhering to the surfaces and suffocating the tree. Species such as the eucalypts have a similar coating to prevent too much transpiration of water in hot, dry weather, while other leaves have fine hairs which achieve the same result by reducing the air flow over the surface. Species such as Japanese maples, which prefer dappled shade, have a very thin skin, or cuticle, which scorches easily when exposed to hot sun.

CUT-AWAY BUD

*Bud scales are formed
from modified leaves*

*Minute embryonic
axillary buds are already
formed*

*The future
apical bud can
be clearly seen*

*A bud is in fact an entire new shoot, complete
with its own apical and axillary buds. It is
tightly compressed and protected by scales.*

▼ With Japanese red maples, the colour in
spring is every bit as impressive as it is in
autumn. The leaves are smaller and much
brighter.

◄ Spruce and needle leaved junipers
produce masses of buds. They open quickly
exposing tight clusters of needles, which
rapidly extend into soft tender shoots.

► Larch buds lose their papery
scales to expose tiny shaving
brushes of new needles. Larch
shoots emerge suddenly from the
centres of these clusters.

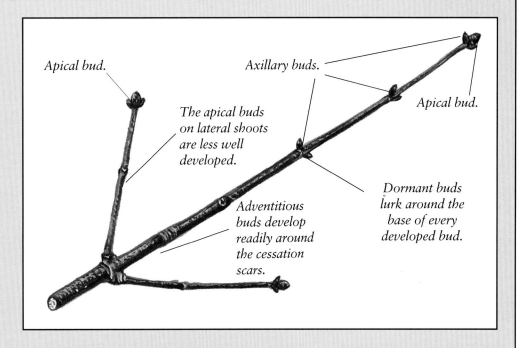

Apical bud.

Axillary buds.

Apical bud.

The apical buds on lateral shoots are less well developed.

Dormant buds lurk around the base of every developed bud.

Adventitious buds develop readily around the cessation scars.

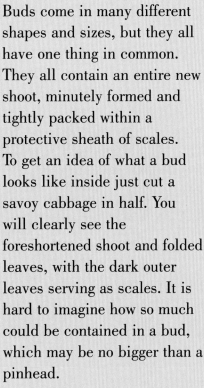

Buds come in many different shapes and sizes, but they all have one thing in common. They all contain an entire new shoot, minutely formed and tightly packed within a protective sheath of scales. To get an idea of what a bud looks like inside just cut a savoy cabbage in half. You will clearly see the foreshortened shoot and folded leaves, with the dark outer leaves serving as scales. It is hard to imagine how so much could be contained in a bud, which may be no bigger than a pinhead.

Terminal or apical buds are formed at the tips of the current year's shoots and are usually the largest since they contain next year's extension growth. These are often flanked by smaller auxiliary buds.

Axillary buds are formed along the length of the shoot, in each leaf axil (the point where the leaf stem, or petiole, joins the shoot), or in the axils of the bud scales. They will either produce the shorter side shoots next year or remain dormant.

Dormant buds are generally axillary buds which failed to open in the year following their formation. They can remain, barely visible, for several years until they are stimulated into growth by pruning, feeding or increased light levels.

Adventitious bud can emerge anywhere on old wood, around pruning cuts or even on roots. They are the tree's response to improved conditions or its method of regeneration after loss of foliage mass. Adventitious buds tend to produce vigorous, sappy shoots.

Growing

Buying and choosing a bonsai is an important factor in how the plant will progress in your home. Growing your own bonsai is another consideration you may decide to look at.

Many newcomers to bonsai begin by being tempted to buy one at a garden centre. The so-called bonsai offered for sale at garden centres are invariably tropical species from the Far or Middle-East. They may have been in stock for some time and be suffering from neglect. Tropical species cannot tolerate our climate, so they must be kept inside for most of the year. This is fine if you can provide a controlled environment, which is not easy. If you are intent on growing bonsai indoors, go to a reputable specialist nursery, whose plants will be well cared for and whose staff will be able to offer good advice. The same advice applies to buying hardy species. Specialist growers know their stuff, so benefit from their experience by asking as many questions as you can. Bonsai people are always glad to help. Meanwhile, the following points will help you get the best value.

▲ When you see trees presented like this you can be fairly confident you are getting good value. They are all healthy, and weed free, and the fertiliser pellets on each pot show they are well cared for.

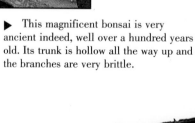

▶ This magnificent bonsai is very ancient indeed, well over a hundred years old. Its trunk is hollow all the way up and the branches are very brittle.

Price

Bonsai are expensive because it takes time to create them by hand, and they are transported half way round the world.

Health

It is best to buy any plant during the growing season so you can be sure it is alive and healthy. Avoid plants with die-back, damaged leaves etc., which may be symptoms of disease. Check the tree is firm in its pot. Hold the trunk and gently try to rock it from side to side. It if moves put it back on the shelf. Check the soil. This should be loose and porous, moist but not waterlogged. The pot must have adequate drainage holes, which are not blocked. There should be no established weeds in the pot. Liverwort and pearlwort are both signs of poor soil.

WHAT TO AVOID!

Neither of these plants could be called a bonsai. The pine (above) is a three-year-old seedling which was pruned once at the end of its second year. The grower wired the trunk to make it look authentic, without altering the shape. Its only potential for bonsai is as raw material, needing to be grown in the ground for many years. The plastic pot reveals the nursery's desire for a fast buck. The little Japanese maple (right) is four years old. Its trunk has been shaped with wire by somebody who has clearly never seen a real tree! There is no way this freak could be turned into a bonsai. The only hope would be to cut the trunk below the first bend and start again.

Appearance

The surface roots should look natural as they emerge from the trunk. The trunk should have a natural shape and taper, with no unsightly scars or graft unions. Avoid bonsai with exaggerated spirals and hairpin bends.

The branches should be evenly distributed around the trunk, the lower ones being thicker than those at the top.

Make sure there are no wire marks on the trunk or branches or, worse still, that there is no wire embedded in the bark.

Aftercare

Always ask the nurseryman about the tree's specific horticultural requirements such as watering, feeding, winter protection and so on, and try to find out when it was last repotted so you know when next to tackle this task.

Garden centre stock

The real essence of bonsai is creating your own, and the most readily available raw material is to be found in garden centres. There is a bewildering range of species and sizes to choose from, which only serves to make the decision more difficult. The following points will help you to make a sensible choice and avoid wasting your money.

What species?

Deciduous or conifer? It doesn't really matter, but bear in mind that, while conifers make more 'instant' bonsai and deciduous species take longer to develop, the latter will reward you with changes in colour and form as the seasons change. It may sound odd, but avoid slow growing or dwarf varieties because they can take a long time to respond to training. The main exceptions to this rule are dwarf spruces which, ironically, make superb bonsai. If you want a flowering species choose one which flowers on the previous year's wood. If the blooms are borne on current year's growth the shoots will need to grow disproportionately long before flowering begins. Test the branches to check that they are supple enough to be shaped by wiring. Finally, decide on a variety which already has small leaves or needles and shows a readiness to produce buds on older wood.

▲ Many garden centre plants are grafted onto sturdier root stocks, causing an unsightly swelling which gets worse as the tree ages. These should be avoided.

▲ At first you may be tempted by 'unusual' trunk shapes like this. But in the case of this plant, unusual means unnatural and it would never make a good bonsai.

▲ The odd weed shows that the plant has become established in the pot, but growth like this liverwort indicates poor drainage and unhealthy roots.

▶ At first sight this dwarf cotoneaster seems ideal for bonsai. Closer inspection reveals that all the branches emerge straight from the soil and there is no trunk, making it useless.

Final choice

Once you decide on the species, you need to select the plant with the most potential. Examine each plant carefully, starting at the base. Expose the surface roots to see if they appear natural. There should be plenty of low branches which still bear foliage close to the trunk. This will present you with many possibilities when you get home and begin to design your bonsai. Don't assume that the existing trunk line will necessarily be the final one, or that the new bonsai will be the same size as the raw material. These options should be carefully considered at your leisure, when you will have time to find the tree's hidden 'soul'.

Growing from seed

If you have the patience there is nothing more rewarding than growing bonsai from seed, regardless of whether you intend to train it from scratch or grow the plant on to form larger raw material. Sowing seed for bonsai is carried out in the same way as for other purposes and is familiar to most people, but the process is outlined here for the complete novice. Extra care is needed when pricking out seedlings.

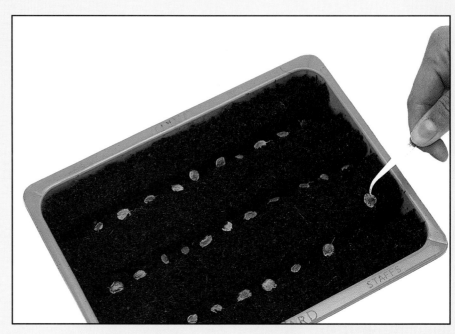

1 Having cleaned your seeds, space them out evenly on a layer of fine compost in a seed tray. Hard seeds germinate better if the shells are chipped with a sharp knife.

4 Cover the seed tray, leaving the ventilation holes fully open. Place the tray outside, where the seeds will be subjected to the natural seasonal changes in the temperature.

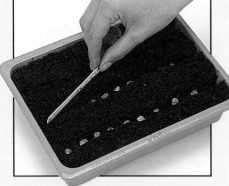

2 Cover the seeds with a layer of compost, to a depth of roughly the thickness of the seeds. Don't press this down, leave it loose so the seeds can breathe.

3 The seed tray should be watered with a spray. Including a copper-based fungicide such as Chestnut compound helps prevent decay as well as 'damping off' of the new seedlings.

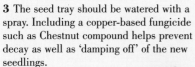

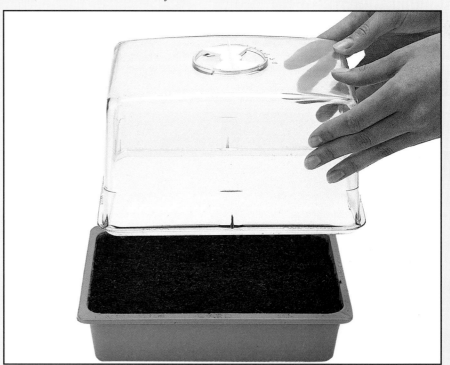

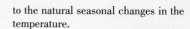

5 Once the seedlings have their first true leaves, gently tease them out. Hold the leaves, not the stem.

6 Use a sharp, sterile blade to cut through the tap root, leaving enough side roots to sustain the seedling.

7 When planting the seedlings in their growing pots, spread the roots radially from the stem. This is the first, essential step in bonsai training, ensuring a good root formation for the future.

8 Cover the roots with bonsai soil. Don't press the soil down as this may damage the tender young roots. Water gently and place the seedlings in a sheltered spot until new growth appears.

Cuttings

The advantage of propagating from cuttings of any type is that you can reproduce the exact characteristics of the parent plant, whereas plants grown from seed may vary. There are three types of cutting appropriate for bonsai: softwood, hardwood and root cuttings.

Softwood cuttings use new growth as the name implies. These should be taken in early summer, and need to be kept in an enclosed, humid atmosphere until they have taken root.

Hardwood cuttings use mature growth and are taken in the autumn, usually using shoots which have grown that year, although some species will root from wood two or more years old.

Root cuttings are suitable for species which naturally throw up shoots, or suckers, from the roots. They can be taken any time between November and April, using roots up to three inches thick.

1 Softwood cuttings are taken in May and June. The lower leaves and the growing tips are cut off using a very sharp blade.

2 Handle the cuttings carefully, and insert them into sandy compost to a depth equal to about a third of their length. It is not necessary to use hormone treatment, although spraying them with systemic fungicide will help prevent decay, thus improving results.

3 Commercial propagators are ideal. They have clear covers with controlled ventilation. Make your own by placing a plastic bag over a pot. Spray cuttings daily until new growth appears.

CHINESE JUNIPER CUTTINGS

Chinese junipers root very easily, although they can take up to a year. Take three inch shoots of last year's growth in June and prepare them as shown.

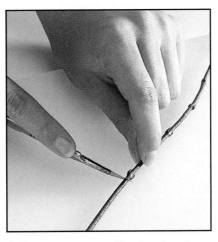

4 There are two types of hardwood cuttings: nodal and heel cuttings. Nodal cuttings should be cut cleanly with a sharp knife, just below a leaf node, or axillary bud.

5 When taking heel cuttings, pull the shoot away from its parent, retaining a sliver of bark, or heel. Trim the heel with a knife.

6 Plant the cuttings to a depth of at least half their length, either in open ground or in a deep pot. Make the holes with a dibber to avoid damaging the ends of the cuttings.

7 When trimming root cuttings use a very sharp blade as their soft back crushes easily. Leaving a few feeder roots will help the cutting on its way.

8 For single-tree styles the root cutting should be planted vertically, making sure it is the right way up!

Growing your own

Two of the most desirable features in any bonsai are mature bark and pronounced taper of the trunk. These properties are always difficult, and often impossible, to achieve when a tree has spent all its life growing slowly in the confines of a shallow bonsai pot.

Traditionally, the most revered specimens were created from stunted plants collected from the mountains of Japan. But nowadays, to do this would be highly irresponsible almost anywhere in the world and certainly illegal in most western countries. The only satisfactory solution is to grow your own raw material in a way which produces all the desirable

1 In full leaf this Siberian elm was just a bush, but in winter the trunk's potential can clearly be seen. Every branch and shoot is cut off leaving just the basic trunk. Prune the top branches selectively so you leave as uniform a taper as possible.

characteristics in as short a time as possible. To do this you need to encourage the lower branches to grow in order to thicken the lower part of the trunk. If the base of the trunk is mulched with straw or leaf mould the bark will swell and crack, making it look even older. The result is a heavy trunk with considerable taper, flaky bark and many old scars – all the characteristics of great age.

The example we have chosen is a Siberian elm which is nine years old and has spent all its life in open ground. Each year it was heavily fed to encourage rapid growth. The top branches were kept trimmed back during each growing season while the lower ones were allowed to grow unchecked for two years at a time. Every two years all branches were removed completely and the whole process repeated.

The drastic root pruning shown here is successful with most elms and trident maple. With other species it is advisable to reduce the roots in stages during successive springs, repotting into a smaller container each time. This elm will be placed in a sheltered position for a few weeks, until new growth appears. It will be fed heavily throughout the next season, so that in a year's time it will be ready for initial styling.

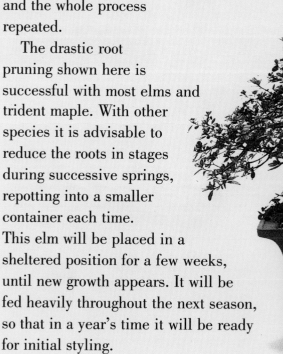

2 Cut the roots as far back as you can, while leaving a few finer roots to sustain the plant until it can grow more. Use a sharp saw as the roots are fibrous and easily tear.

3 Plant the trunk quite deep in a generous sized container filled with good bonsai soil.

4 Cover the remaining roots well to conserve moisture. New growth will appear in mid summer.

Reducing taller trees

Some people prefer to grow very large bonsai but are unable to find suitable raw material growing in open ground, and are unwilling to spend the required number of years to grow their own. The only alternative is to acquire a suitable plant from a tree nursery. These trees are intended for planting in parks, streets or large gardens and are grown in the ground for a number of years before being established in containers prior to sale. When seeking out such material make sure it is well established in its container; moss and weeds growing on the soil are a good indication of this.

3 Use typwriter correction fluid or paint to mark the trunk.

1 This twelve feet tall hornbeam (Carpinus betulus) was brought from a landscape tree nursery, and was chosen because it had plenty of low branches.

2 Choose a branch for the new leader and make the cut diagonally downwards from this, towards a lower branch on the opposite side of the trunk.

4 Carve the wound gradually up to the line, without tearing the bark. Hollowing out the heartwood a little will help the wound to heal flat, resulting in an almost invisible scar. Then seal the entire wound with cut paste, making sure that the edges are well covered.

5 Seal the entire wound with cut paste, making sure that the edges are well covered.

6 The lower branches should now be kept trimmed to encourage fine twigs, while the top can grow freely.

Shaping with wire

Wiring is the most fundamental process in bonsai training, allowing the accurate positioning of branches and shoots. The principle is simple but the skill does take a little time to acquire. Wire of a suitable gauge is coiled around a branch or shoot. The two can then be bent and manoeuvred into the desired position, and the wire will hold the branch in place. After a period of growth has taken place, the branch will set in that position and the wire can be removed. The time taken for this to happen varies from one species to another. Conifers, especially junipers, may take several years to set, during which time the wire may need to be removed and reapplied several times to avoid damaging the bark. Some deciduous species may set in a matter of a few weeks. Older, stiffer branches will also take longer, and you may have to bend them little by little every few weeks until the desired position is achieved. Every plant is an individual, and it is only with experience that you will learn just how far you can go before snapping the branch, so take it easy at first. Before you embark on your first wiring exercise you should practice the technique on a twig or branch from a garden shrub, preferably a species similar to the one you have chosen for your bonsai.

▲ The branches on this old shimpaku juniper from Japan would have been wired into position many years ago.

See how thick the wire needs to be, and how far the branch will bend without breaking.

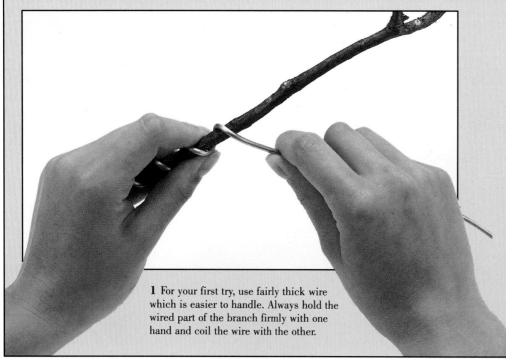

1 For your first try, use fairly thick wire which is easier to handle. Always hold the wired part of the branch firmly with one hand and coil the wire with the other.

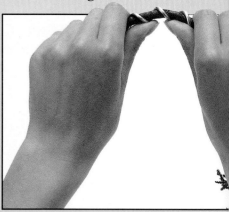

2 When you bend the branch, do it gradually. Spread your hands so you hold as much of the branch as possible and use both thumbs as leverage points. Once bent, the wire should hold the branch in position. If the branch springs back, the wire is too thin, if it cuts the bark, it is too tight.

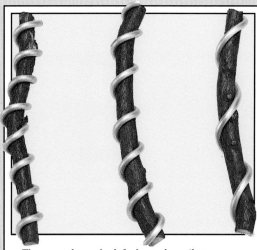

The example on the left shows the coils too close together. On the right the coils are too far apart. The example in the centre shows ideal wiring.

3 When wiring long branches, reduce the thickness of the wire as the branch diameter decreases. Overlap the different thicknesses by two or three turns.

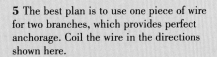

5 The best plan is to use one piece of wire for two branches, which provides perfect anchorage. Coil the wire in the directions shown here.

6 It is also best to use one piece of wire for forked branches. Make sure you coil it in opposite directions on each branch, otherwise the wire on the first branch will uncoil as you work on the second one.

4 When wiring a side branch, anchor the wire by coiling it around the trunk. Always take it through the fork of the branch as shown.

CLAMPS

Sometimes you may want to create a sharp bend, or alter the direction of a really thick branch or trunk, where no amount of wire would have any effect. In such cases special clamps like this can be employed. They are available in a variety of sizes, the largest one being capable of bending a conifer branch over one inch thick. Care must be taken to cushion the bark against the considerable pressure applied by the clamp. Avoid trying to create too severe a bend in one go – it is much better to give the clamp an extra turn every week or so until the desired position is reached.

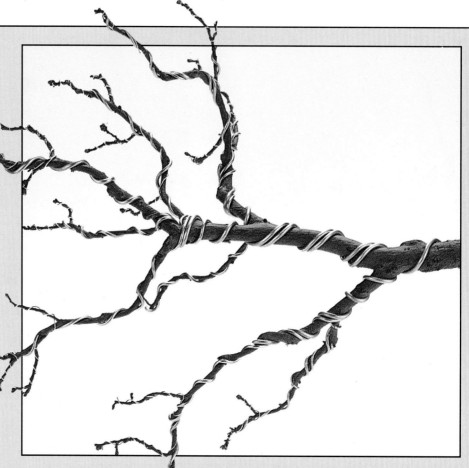

1 A plan view of a fully wired deciduous branch. Note how the side branches are fanned out like spread fingers, and how straight lines are avoided.

2 'Side view of the same branch. It is important to build height on the branches of deciduous trees, as well as width. There is plenty of space between each shoot for future growth.

3 Pine branches are wired to a different shape. The side branches should cascade slightly from the main limb, forming a low dome. The tip of each shoot is wired to point upwards.

5 If the wire stays on too long it will cut right into the bark like this. Remove it in good time and, if the branch hasn't set, rewire it, coiling in the opposite direction.

REMOVING WIRE

Wire can be expensive, so it is tempting to unwind it once it has served its purpose, in order to use it another time. However this is a risky business since it is much easier to damage the bark, or even snap the branch, when working in reverse. The branch will have swollen so the wire will be tighter than when you first applied it, and will naturally be full of kinks, making it difficult to manipulate.

It is much safer to snip the wire away using wire cutters which cut right up to the tip of the jaws. Custom-made Japanese bonsai wire cutters are designed for this purpose, but can be quite expensive. To start with, good quality electrical wire cutters will do the job just as well if you choose the tool carefully. You will need the long-handled type to enable you to reach awkward places. Any damage to the bark caused by the cutters will be superficial and will heal much quicker than damage caused through careless uncoiling.

If you are worried about the unnecessary expense of 'wasting' wire in this way, ask yourself this question: what is the most valuable to you, a few inches of wire or a developing bonsai which you have laboured over for hours and nurtured for years?

4 A plan view of a juniper branch, shaped in the traditional way for the formal upright style. Note the triangular shape and how the side branches are positioned alternately. On junipers and pines, stripping old foliage like this allows light to stimulate back budding. For some curious reason, the wire itself also seems to have a similar affect.

Branch pruning

When a branch is pruned it will inevitably leave a scar. With full-sized trees the wound will normally heal rapidly and any resulting disfiguration will be of little or no consequence. However, since bonsai grow more slowly the healing process is slower as well, so it needs all the help it can get. The first technique shows you how to execute simple pruning, where a small to medium sized branch is removed. The second shows how to use a larger wound to your advantage, by hollowing it out and turning it into an interesting feature.

General points

Always use very sharp tools, which should ideally be sterilised by immersing them in methylated spirit for a few minutes. This is especially important when pruning away diseased wood. The cambium layer (between the bark and the heartwood) must be sealed against frost, water and drying wind. If left exposed it may die back, increasing the size of the wound and delaying the healing process. Never use horticultural bitumen-based sealants. These will dry hard and will be impossible to remove from the surrounding bark without causing disfiguration and damage to the tree. Feed the tree well after drastic pruning to speed up the healing process.

1 If you don't have any bonsai tools some sharp secateurs will do. Leave a small stub at first, rather than attempting to cut right up to the trunk. If you do have special branch pruners, use them to finish off the cut as close to the trunk as possible.

2 Clean up the edges of the wound with a very sharp knife. Ragged edges heal unevenly and are likely to harbour fungal spores which may infect the whole tree.

3 Seal the wound thoroughly, especially around the edges. If you don't have any special bonsai sealant, try mixing a little olive oil with grafting wax or children's modelling clay.

DISGUISING WOUNDS

Sometimes it is necessary to prune away really heavy branches, causing scars which would normally take many years to heal. Even then, they might be too large to be in proportion with the scale of the rest of the bonsai.

You can turn these large scars to your advantage by hollowing out the wound, right through to the heartwood. If carried out with care this can result in a natural looking feature which will add age and character to the trunk. You can make the hollow as deep as you like, since the heartwood is essentially dead, so long as the sapwood and cambium are intact.

Maintenance pruning

Each year your bonsai will throw out new shoots from the buds created in the leaf axils during the previous growing season. It will only take a few weeks for these shoots to outgrow the design of the tree and make it look very scruffy. In a developing or semi-mature bonsai these shoots can be allowed to grow to six or seven leaves before they are cut back. Allowing them this period of free growth thickens the parent branches and trunk and builds up a general vigour in the tree. If allowed to grow too long they will sap the strength from the finer growth and will quickly kill it off. New shoots will emerge from the buds in the remaining leaf axils. Any wayward shoots, or those which are destined to become new branches, should be wired at this stage. However, in established bonsai this annual growth will need to be cut back during the dormant season to allow the next season's growth room to extend before outgrowing the design. Over the seasons this constant 'clip-and-grow' technique will reward you with a much-forked branch structure, with all the characteristics of an ancient tree.

Here we show how to approach the winter pruning of trees with alternate and opposite leaves – in this case English elm and Japanese maple. Always remember to prune to a bud which points in the direction you want the new growth to take. It is possible to style a bonsai entirely by pruning if you have the patience. The best time to do your winter pruning is late in the season, before the buds swell but after the worst of the weather is over. The setback to the tree caused by pruning off fattening buds is slight. But prolonged periods of frost could do severe damage to a newly-pruned bonsai.

2 Every few years it is necessary to prune away older growth to prevent overcrowding and to maintain neat foliage pads. Finally, cut back all shoots to one or two buds.

3 Like the maple, this elm has grown some long shoots which need to be pruned first. This is also a good time to prune off any stubs and dead shoots. Note how each shoot has been pruned to a bud facing in the direction the new growth is required.

1 During the previous growing season this maple produced a few long shoots. The first step is to cut them back to a short shoot.

Summary pinching

Once the branch structure has become established there should be enough new shoots appearing each spring, bearing sufficient foliage to sustain the tree without necessarily allowing any extension growth. Extension growth draws the energy from the rest of the tree, concentrating it in the growing tips. This starves the fine inner twigs of nutrients and the additional foliage prevents them gaining adequate light. The result is that the fine twigs die. First we have to build and refine this tracery of fine twigs. Once this has been done the resulting foliage pads must be kept trimmed and in balance with the design. Both these ends are achieved by pinching out the tips of all new growth as it appears.

Different species grow in different ways, and the following techniques have been developed to accommodate the five most common growth patterns. With broadleaved trees new shoots will emerge from the buds in the remaining leaf axils.

In pines new buds will form at the point at which the shoot is pinched, as well as further back on older growth. Junipers will throw out new growth from any branch or shoot which bears foliage, and need constant pinching throughout the season.

1 Spruce buds open to form tiny, bright green tufts which should be plucked before they have fully elongated. Don't do the whole tree at one go, spread the job over two weeks.

2 As pine buds begin to grow they elongate, forming 'candles' which should have up to two thirds snapped off before the needles develop. Twist and bend at the same time.

3 Junipers produce prolific new growth. This growth is distinguished by its lighter colour. Hold the fan of foliage in one hand and pull out all extending growth with the finger and thumb of the other.

4 Zelkovas and other alternate-leaved species produce new leaves one at a time at the shoot tips. This leaf, and the minute bud at its base, should be pinched out, using tweezers if necessary.

5 Maples produce new leaves in pairs borne on a short extending shoot. Both leaves should be pinched out, together with the tiny developing bud nestled between them.

Leaf pruning

This is the ultimate refinement technique which is only suitable for broadleaved deciduous species. It results in a very fine twig formation, tiny leaves and enhanced autumn colour the year it is applied.

Since this technique causes a certain amount of stress to the tree it should only be carried out every three years or so, and only on trees which are in good health and vigour. For this reason its use is normally restricted to bonsai which are in preparation for exhibition. The ideal time for leaf pruning is early summer, as soon as the spring growth has hardened.

The principle is similar to shoot pruning and pinching, in that the reduction of foliage encourages new side growth to take place. But because the foliage is totally removed the tree undergoes a 'false autumn' and next year's growth develops this year. This means that there will be a much greater number of new shoots than existed before, bearing correspondingly more leaves. Since the tree can only support – and only requires – a fixed volume of foliage, these leaves will be greatly reduced in size. Also, since these leaves only have half a season to live they will be in better condition resulting in brighter colour.

1 This shohin field maple received a merit award from Saburo Kato, president of the World Bonsai Federation. Being small, it needs regular leaf pruning.

2 Cut just below the leaf, leaving the petiole, or leaf stalk, intact. This prevents excessive 'bleeding'.

4 The petioles which remain on the tree will fall as soon as the new leaves start to emerge. After a week or two the new leaves emerge.

3 Leaf pruning also presents an ideal opportunity to check the progress of the branch structure.

5 Less than a month later the tree has grown a full crop of small, brightly-coloured leaves, borne on short shoots

Creating Styles

The main aim of bonsai is to create a tree-like form in miniature. This can be anything from a precise replica of a classic parkland beech to the image of a gnarled and weather beaten mount-top juniper, which can be almost abstract in design. There is an infinite variety of tree shapes in nature which are imitated in bonsai.

INFORMAL UPRIGHT – MOYOGI

This is a variation on the formal upright style but is much easier to create. The rules for the branch structure are the same but the trunk may have any number of curves, both from left to right and from front to back. The branches should ideally grow from the outside of the curves and never on the inside as this creates a shock to the eye. The apex should lean towards the front. The illustration shows the ideal form, but any number of variations are perfectly acceptable.

FORMAL UPRIGHT STYLE – CHOKKAN

As the name implies, this is the most formalised of all styles. The trunk must be ramrod straight and bolt upright, tapering uniformly from base to tip. The branches should be arranged alternately either side of the trunk with every third branch to the rear. The branches should diminish in thickness and in length from the lowest one upwards, and should be either horizontal or sloping downwards.

SEMI-CASCADE – HAN-KENGAI

Both this style and the cascade style (overleaf) depict trees clinging to a cliff face, where they are beaten by snow, wind and rockfalls. The trunk should have dramatic curves and taper, and the branches should ideally also cascade from the trunk. Tradition states that the inverted 'apex' should be directly below the centre of the trunk. The one unbreakable rule is that the lowest point must be below the rim of the pot, but not its base.

SLANTING – SHAKAN
Another variation on the formal upright
style, except that it is not upright. The trunk
is usually straight-ish, although it may have
a gentle curve or two. The placement of the
branches needs to be carefully thought out
in order to stabilise the design and to
prevent the tree looking as if it is about to
fall over.

WINDSWEPT – FUKINAGASHI
Although this is one of the more naturalistic
styles, it is also one of the most dramatic.
The aim is to capture the dynamic shape
and movement of a tree living high in the
mountains or on a clifftop, where it is
constantly exposed to high prevailing winds.
There are no rules governing the trunk
shape or location of branches, but in spite
of this freedom this is one of the most
difficult styles to create successfully.

▲ An example of an Informal Upright tree

ROOT-OVER-ROCK – SEKIJOJU

In rocky terrain the scarce soil is constantly being eroded, exposing the rocks and the roots of the trees growing amongst them. This style depicts such a tree whose roots, as they thicken, cling to any rocks beneath them. The tree itself can be of any style, although broom and formal upright styles look out of place. The most important factor is that the roots should cling tightly to the rock and should have a mature texture.

BROOM – HOKIDACHI

This style was modelled on the natural habit of the zelkova and is seldom successfully used for other than related species, since it works best with trees bearing alternate foliage. All branches should emerge from the top of a straight trunk and fork at regularly diminishing intervals until a network of fine shoots at the tips forms an even-domed crown.

ROOTS-ON-ROCK – ISHITSUKI

The tree itself may follow any style, the significance is that a rock is used instead of a pot, with the roots growing in a crevice or hollow. The rock may stand in a shallow dish of soil or, better still, in a water tray. Mixed plantings of pines with red maples or dwarf quince and azalea are particularly successful.

DRIFTWOOD – SHARIMIKI

Echoing the natural appearance of mountain junipers, which produce areas of bare, sun-bleached wood as they age, this style is seldom successfully created from other species. The focal point is the beautiful and dramatic shapes of the grain in the exposed wood. These shapes may be natural but are more often elaborately carved and then bleached and preserved with lime-sulphur. The foliage masses, although acknowledging some of the rules of other styles, serve more as a foil or frame to the driftwood.

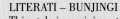

LITERATI – BUNJINGI

This style is reminiscent of ancient pines which tend to shed their lower branches as they get old. It gets its name from the calligraphic style of ancient Chinese artists.

CASCADE – KENGAI

The difference between this style and the semi-cascade is that here the trunk must fall below the base of the pot. All other criteria are the same. Good cascades are rare because of the difficulty in maintaining vigour in the lower parts of the tree, opposing its natural urge to grow upwards.

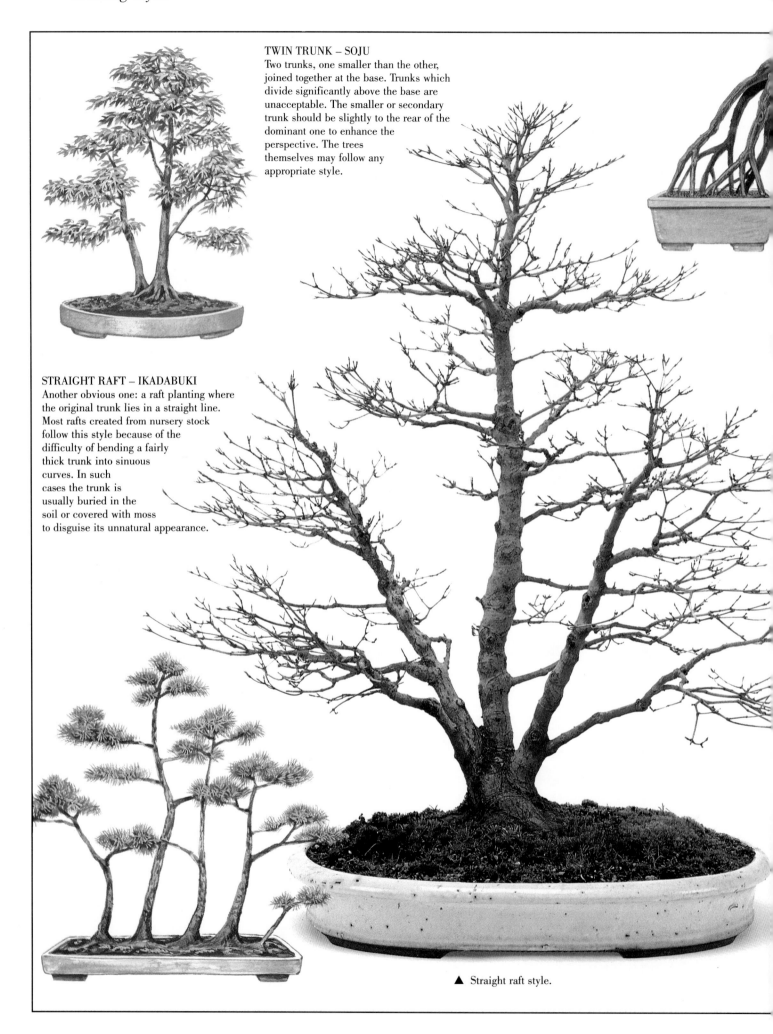

TWIN TRUNK – SOJU
Two trunks, one smaller than the other, joined together at the base. Trunks which divide significantly above the base are unacceptable. The smaller or secondary trunk should be slightly to the rear of the dominant one to enhance the perspective. The trees themselves may follow any appropriate style.

STRAIGHT RAFT – IKADABUKI
Another obvious one: a raft planting where the original trunk lies in a straight line. Most rafts created from nursery stock follow this style because of the difficulty of bending a fairly thick trunk into sinuous curves. In such cases the trunk is usually buried in the soil or covered with moss to disguise its unnatural appearance.

▲ Straight raft style.

EXPOSED ROOT – NEGARI
Most of us have driven down country lanes where the steep banks either side have been washed away to expose the roots of ancient beech or pine, and this style is based on such cases. The roots, which must have mature bark and interesting shapes, add a dramatic, rugged appearance, so the design of the tree itself should echo this.

OTHERS
Other bonsai classes relate to size: Shohin are up to ten inches or so tall, and Mame, or miniature bonsai, are defined as 'being able to sit comfortably in the palm of the hand'.

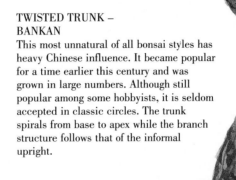

CLUMB – KABUDACHI
Any (odd) number of trunks, which must be in a variety of sizes, all growing on the same roots. This may either be created from suckers (shoots arising naturally from the roots) or by cutting off a thick trunk at the base and using the new shoots which spring up from the stump. The trees can be any style. The horticultural advantage of using a lump rather than separate plants is that the 'trees' do not compete for water and nutrients.

TWISTED TRUNK – BANKAN
This most unnatural of all bonsai styles has heavy Chinese influence. It became popular for a time earlier this century and was grown in large numbers. Although still popular among some hobbyists, it is seldom accepted in classic circles. The trunk spirals from base to apex while the branch structure follows that of the informal upright.

SINUOUS RAFT – NETSUNANARI
As the name suggests, this is a raft planting where the original horizontal trunk has attractive, snake-like curves and is exposed to show this feature to its best advantage. It is even acceptable for the old trunk to be above the ground in places. The individual trees may follow any style.

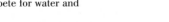

GROUP – YOSE-UE
This style may incorporate any number of trunks from seven up to as many as you like. The main interest is in the interplay between the trunks, which should be of different sizes and should be arranged to give the impression of depth and perspective. No three trunks should form a straight line and no trunk should be obscured by another when viewed from the front.

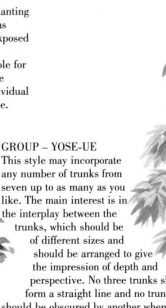

Cuttings

Seedlings and cuttings are free and easy to come by, so they are ideal material for your first attempts at creating bonsai. If the result is not too good it doesn't really matter, you will probably have other plants ready to replace the initial failure. If, on the other hand, the result is satisfactory you will have a bonsai that will improve as time goes by with the right care and attention. We have repotted this cutting to complete the demonstration. You should ideally wait until the following spring, to allow the plant time to regain strength. Whatever species you choose, seedling or cutting, the plant should be growing vigorously before you attempt any pruning or wiring. For this sequence we selected a two-year-old cutting of a juniper, Junipers squamata meyerii, because its compact foliage enables us to create an almost instant bonsai. With deciduous species you will have to build up the shape over two or three years.

1 Clear all the foliage and small shoots from the trunk, leaving the larger branches. Try to avoid leaving opposite branches.

2 Don't let the size of the original plant dictate the eventual size of the bonsai. Here we are cutting off one of the twin leaders, leaving a side shoot to form a branch.

3 The other leader is now shortened. This time a side shoot is left to become the new leader. Working this way, we are increasing trunk taper, making the tree appear older.

4 To start wiring the trunk, take a sturdy piece of wire and anchor it by pushing it into the soil close to the trunk. Find a spot where you will not damage any roots.

5 Hold the trunk and wire together firmly and begin to coil. Hold close to the point where you are coiling and move your hand along the trunk as you progress.

6 Next wire the branches, using one piece of wire for two branches. Wire right to the tip of each branch.

7 Grasp as much of the trunk as possible to spread the pressure and bend it into the desired shape. Introduce some curves from side front to back as well as from side to side.

8 Bend the branches down, making sure there are a few at the back. Bend close to the trunk. Clear any growth facing downwards.

Seedlings

Nowadays most bonsai are created by reducing larger plants or by growing branches onto pre-formed trunks. However, there is still a very important place for growing bonsai straight from seed. It helps you to learn about the growth patterns of each species and makes you more aware of the structure of trees. But most importantly, by growing bonsai from seed you can create an almost perfect little tree on a very small scale, without the need for heavy pruning scars, jins and so on. Being able to display a tiny unblemished and well formed bonsai that you grew from seed is a most satisfying and rewarding achievement.

1 This typical hawthorn seedling is beginning its third summer. Note the position and angle of the cut.

2 After three months the spurs have become strong shoots. Two will become branches, the third a new leader.

3 Now the trunk can be shaped. Bend from the back to front as well as side to side.

4 The branches have been wired spread evenly around the trunk and lowered to a horozontal position.

5 Shortening the stronger branches encourages new ones to form as well as promoting side growth on the remaining ones.

Cotoneaster

One of my favourite species for bonsai is Cotoneaster. The tiny leaves are dark, glossy green, they bear minute pink-white flowers in spring and the bright red berries stay on the plant from late summer right through the winter. Some varieties, like horozontal, which we have chosen here, are deciduous, giving the added bonus of autumn golds and reds. The growth is symmetrical and entirely predictable, producing a herring-bone pattern of branches and twigs – ideal for bonsai training into almost any style.

Garden centre plants tend to be well fed and watered but they live fairly close together. This encourages long, vigorous shoots which we are going to use to our advantage in this exercise by creating a cascade style.

Because it is against the tree's nature to grow downwards it will channel more energy to the crown at the expense of the tip of the cascade. To compensate for this you should select a vigorous branch for the cascade and keep the top well thinned out. Spray foliar feed on the lower parts regularly and only use a foilar fertiliser sparingly.

1 This cotoneaster is typical of garden centre stock, with strong branches growing in all directions, but no discernable trunk. By tilting it to one side, its potential for a cascade style becomes apparent.

It is quite common for extreme cascades to be laid on their backs for much of the time and only to be stood upright for watering. This can also help counter the tree's compulsion to grow upwards, but it does have disadvantages. The pot may not drain too well in this position and the leaves will turn to face the light, so they look odd when the bonsai is the right way up. It takes a day or two for the leaves to re-adjust to their normal position.

2 The essence of a good cascade style is to make the trunk begin its cascade as close to the base as possible, so it is cut right back to the lowest pair of heavy branches.

3 One remaining branch becomes the new leader and the other is shortened to form a low, stunted crown.

4 Rub off cluttered shoots and wire the new trunk from base to tip, taking care not to crush any small branches beneath the wire.

5 Make the bends in the trunk as sharp as possible, reflecting the tortuous conditions suffered by natural cascading trees in the mountains. The bends should be made from front to back as well as from side to side, and should be tighter towards the tip of the trunk.

6 When you are satisfied with the trunk line you can decide which side branches to keep. Try to make these emerge from the outside of a bend in the trunk. The trunk should be cleaned of all other shoots and tufts of foliage.

7 The branches should cascade in the same way as the trunk, with similar curves, but on a smaller scale. Note how the sparse branches in the stunted crown also cascade, giving unity to the design.

8 Leave a few short stubs to serve as anchorage points for the wire when you prune. This is kinder to the plant than anchoring the wire round the trunk. ,

9 Once the tree is planted in a proper cascade pot the final adjustments can be made to the branches. It will now grow away vigorously, especially at the extreme top and bottom, so regular pruning will be needed to keep the foliage pads neat. In time more branches may be pruned.

Cedar

The Literati style, although found frequently in nature, gets its name from the fact that the trunk shapes were originally inspired by the brush strokes of ancient Chinese scribes. This is the oldest style of bonsai and was established long before it became popular in Japan. It is the original link between horticulture and art. In nature this style is invariably limited to exposed, mountain conifers such as Scots pine, larch or spruce, which naturally shed lower branches as they mature. Very rarely does one find a literati deciduous tree of any beauty. The essence of the design is the trunk line,

which should have taper and should present many changes of direction. The branches are limited to the uppermost portion of the trunk and foliage is kept to a minimum – just sufficient to maintain the tree's health. In this case we are using a garden centre cedar whose initial attraction was the long lower branch, which eventually becomes the leader. It is amazing how often the removal of most of the trunk, and the selection of a lower branch to take its place, can create ancient-looking and dramatic effects. Only repot at the same sitting if you're working in spring, otherwise wait until next year.

1 We chose this Atlantic cedar because of the potential offered by the long, low branch.

2 The surface roots of this plant were buried deep in the pot. The tough elastic net, used by the nursery when transplanting, has to be disentangled and cut away.

3 The obvious first step is to remove the unwanted upper trunk, leaving a stub to form a jin later. Using a branch as the new leader increases taper and creates a sharp bend.

4 Next the short spurs and tufts of foliage need to be cleaned from the trunk, and the first quarter of each branch. Then you can select which branches to keep and which to prune.

5 The stub of the original trunk is jinned and the trunk and branches are wired. The essence of literati is trunk line and sparse foliage, so only a few branches remain.

6 When shaping the trunk, aim for a combination of sharp bends and gradual curves. Try not to make them predictable, and remember to work in three dimensions, not just two.

7 Having established the basic trunk and branch structure, the final tidying up takes place. Any downward-facing buds or shoots must be removed.

▲ Three months later the tree has put on considerable growth and has already had its first pinching. As the tree develops, the bottom branches will be removed.

8 Fortunately the roots are in excellent condition, as you can see. Because this tree leans considerably, it needs to be wired firmly into the pot.

Juniper

1 This Chinese juniper outgrew its space in a neighbour's rock garden. The root ball is wrapped in netting to keep it intact while we are working out the tree.

As the name implies, this style is inspired by trees found growing on cliff-tops, where they are shaped by constant exposure to prevailing winds. Although the principles behind the design are simple it can be difficult to arrive at a totally convincing result and much depends on the potential of the raw material. The most suitable species for this style are conifers, since the foliage pads have cleaner outlines and the growth can be precisely controlled. With deciduous trees the larger leaves face all directions, ruining the effect, particularly on smaller bonsai. Choose a plant which already has a tendency to grow towards one side, or has one side branch showing potential, which can become the main trunk. Keep the trunk and the first half to two-thirds of the branch line clear of foliage. In nature winds not only shape the branches, they also strip young shoots and only allow new growth at the tips, where the force of the wind is broken by the rest of the tree. This process must be imitated by the bonsai artist in the years that follow the initial styling. This will inevitably lead to over-extended growth, so every few years it will be necessary to cut the foliage pads back as far as possible and re-grow them. As a result you will create an ever more angular and battered looking branch structure which will add to the beauty of your bonsai. Never be afraid to adjust the design as time passes by removing or jinning branches, or creating sharis on the trunk. The more 'damage' you can create on this style of bonsai, the more convincing it will eventually become.

2 From underneath the main trunk line is more visible. Start by removing all dead shoots and weak, spindly branches.

3 The trunkline is now clear, but there's more pruning to do yet. Windswept trees shed branches as they grow, retaining a few on the lee side.

5 Having wired the remaining branches, they should all be shaped to follow the wind-blown sweep of the trunk, with similar curves, but on a decreasing scale.

4 The unwanted branches have been removed and some of the thicker ones jinned. Now the tree is beginning to take shape. The smaller trunk on the right may come in useful, so it has been left for the time being. The tree is held at the correct angle by an upturned pot.

6 All downward-facing shoots must now be cut off to emphasise the flowing branch lines, characteristic of the windswept style.

7 Note how the foliage pads are being trimmed to a narrow wedge shape – another divide to enhance the illusion of a tree which is subjected to strong prevailing winds.

Siberian elm

Here we have used a Siberian elm grown from seed, which has been growing in open ground for six years before being potted up in early spring a year ago. These are vigorous trees and are ideal for this method of styling. What we are doing here in effect is building a bonsai. We start by developing a good trunk with an interesting line and pronounced taper. The next step is to add the branches. As you can see we have plenty of choice. Many of the older branches are too thick to bend next to the trunk so we will concentrate on the young, thinner ones. The best time to tackle a project like this is in mid-summer, while the tree still has plenty of time to put on a lot more growth before autumn. If you do it too late in the year the new growth will not be fully hardened before the frosts begin and it will wither. If you try this while the tree is dormant frost may enter the hairline cracks caused when the branches are bent and this may result in die-back of entire branches, which means back to square one!

When positioning the basic branch structure you should avoid straight lines (unless you are producing a formal upright style) and try to bend the branch at each point where a side shoot emerges. Remember to introduce vertical curves as well as horizontal ones. Feed the tree well to

encourage new growth but reduce the nitrogen content towards late summer in order to harden off any tender young shoots. Allow all the new shoots which emerge from the branches to grow unchecked in order to thicken the host branches. Apply the wire fairly loosely because the branches will thicken and set rapidly. Check the wiring after three weeks and then every few days after that. As soon as it appears too tight renew it immediately.

Next spring the long shoots can be pruned back and selected ones wired into position to form the secondary branches. New growth from these should be allowed to extend to six or seven leaf nodes, and then trimmed back to two or three. These, too, can be loosely wired into position. Feeding heavily will mean that you will need to repeat this 'grow and clip' cycle several times throughout the season. In a year or two this tree can be planted in a display pot and the refinement stage can begin.

1 Many of these branches are too thick to be of use. They would tend to split away from the trunk when bent. They will be cut off completely; the rest will be shortened.

3 Selected shoots are shortened and wired into position. Any over-long side shoots are also shortened to encourage bushy growth. It is a good idea to introduce quite exaggerated curves in the branches at this stage as they will become less pronounced as the branches thicken.

▲ Before the end of the season the foliage pads are developing well. Next spring the tree will be planted in a proper bonsai pot.

Scots pine

1 The raw material. It has plenty of branches plus a small, secondary trunk. The main trunk forks about halfway up, and the thickest fork is removed first.

2 Pines always produce whorls of branches like these. If allowed to remain they form thick 'knuckles' and disfigure the trunk. All but one or two branches must be pruned.

3 Most branches have been pruned, leaving only those which are needed for the design. The front, which displays the best trunk shape, is marked with a pencil stuck in the pot.

Most big garden centres, especially those who specialise in landscaping, will stock large container-grown trees and shrubs. These can offer tremendous potential and are, surprisingly, rather easier to work on than you may think at first. Here we have chosen a variety of Scots pine, Pinus sylvestris nana. It has a compact growth pattern, readily throws out buds on old wood and naturally produces very small needles. Other similar varieties are Beauvronensis and Waterii. Steer clear of varieties which have long needles and coarse growth. Although Japanese pine bonsai are grown in many styles: literati, cascade, driftwood etc., the vast majority of commercial trees seem to be stocky, thick-trunked informal or formal uprights. These full triangular shapes are more reminiscent of young pine trees in the west. If you look at the pines in your neighbourhood you will discover they have a style all of their own, approaching literati sometimes, but relatively straight-trunked with cascading branches. This is the style we are aiming for here. This sort of operation can be carried out any time between early summer, when new needles are hardening off, and early autumn. If you try this too late in the year the tiny wounds caused by severe bending of the branches will not have time to seal themselves against winter frosts and die-back may result. You don't have to complete a task like this in one sitting; take several weeks over it if you like. In fact the tree will thank you if you do since a staged operation is less traumatic. Having completed the styling exercise wait until the following year before you repot. If by then the tree still seems weak wait another year. Check the wire regularly and replace it when it becomes too tight, coiling it in the opposite direction.

4 The secondary trunk is positioned so it is visible from the front. All old needles are removed to make wiring easier and to encourage back budding before wiring the lower left branch.

5 Wires are not sufficient to hold the secondary trunk in place, so a tourniquet fixed to the pot's rim takes the strain. This can be tightened a little every few weeks if necessary.

6 Thick branches can be made to bend closer to the trunk by gently splitting them away from the trunk and using thick wire, or a stone, to hold the slit open. The wound must be sealed.

7 These fine white strands are mycelium of a mycorrhyzal fungus which helps the tree absorb nutrients from the soil. If you find this in a pot, keep it. Root aphids look similar at first, but the insects are clearly visible.

8 After more thinning, the secondary branches are wired into position. The bonsai is now taking shape, but there is more to do. Every shoot must be wired to face outwards or upwards, to form domed pads.

Special Projects

Once you have gained a little experience and confidence, it is fun to move on to other projects in bonsai. Do not worry if some of your first attempts fail, because it all helps you to understand what nature can and cannot do.

Beech group

Most species can be used for creating bonsai groups and the results can be almost instantly satisfying. The main effect is achieved by the interplay between the trunks of different thicknesses and lines, and the actual branch structure is less important than it is with a single tree. Successful groups can be created from young, spindly plants which would normally be little or no use as single trees, so this is a good way to utilise seedlings or cuttings which you would otherwise discard. We have chosen some rooted beech cuttings which were intended for hedging. This type of raw material is usually sold in large numbers, so it is very cheap, and there is always plenty to choose from. Other hedging stock includes hawthorn, elm, privet, field maple etc. It is important to select plants of different heights and thicknesses in order to create perspective and interest. Stick to odd numbers; they are easier to compose (the Japanese actually have a superstitious aversion to even numbers) and avoid the temptation to use too many plants at first. A group of more than nine or so becomes a forest, which is subject to slightly different aesthetic principles. Create your group in early spring, and keep it in a humid and well ventilated place, such as an open-ended polytunnel, until the roots are established and growth is evident. Little

1 These beech cuttings are not particularly inspiring at first sight, but their different thicknesses and lines are just what we need to create a group.

2 Cut away the long roots with sharp scissors, leaving as many fine feeder roots as possible.

3 Work a sticky mixture of equal parts of clay and fine peat between the roots, and mould them into a ball.

4 The clay balls keep the trees in position while they are being arranged in the pot. Start with the tallest tree, just off centre, and place the two next tallest either side.

5 Build up the design tree by tree, adding the smaller ones at the sides and rear to create perspective. Leaning the trees away from the centre gives the illusion of greater size.

6 When the arrangement is complete add soil between the clay balls. Dry soil is easier to apply as it does not stick to the wet clay.

7 Carefully work the soil into all the spaces between the rootballs using a pencil. Ensure that all the spaces are filled with soil.

8 You can complete the picture by 'landscaping' the soil surface with different kinds of moss and grit. Water the pot and moss thoroughly first, and avoid pressing the moss down too hard.

or no wiring should be necessary since the foliage will hide the branches and will merely act as a visual foil to the trunk arrangement. Any branches growing towards the centre of the group should be removed and from then on all you will need to do is prune new growth and thin out cluttered shoots.

9 The new planing is already pleasing to the eye. Note how the trees at the edges have been pruned so each apex sweeps outwards.

Informal upright maple

Once a young tree has been allowed to thicken to about half an inch or so it becomes virtually impossible to bend. What's more, if allowed to grow freely it will lack taper and thus become useless as it is for bonsai purposes. However, you can still take advantage of the tree's natural resilience to

1 The roots of this newly-dug Japanese maple are wrapped to preserve moisture while the trunk is cut directly above the bottom two branches or dormant buds.

create an informal upright style with severe taper, by employing this 'prune-and-grow' technique. Any deciduous species can be used but Japanese maples are by far the most successful. The fact that they have opposite leaves, and therefore produce new shoots opposite each other, creates a mechanical pattern. This enables you to position the branches exactly on the outside of bends in the trunk – which is aesthetically more pleasing and also means that the branch structure will echo the trunk's angular form. The tree we have chosen here is five years old and has been grown in open ground for the past three years. In common with most trees of this age, it has retained two small, weak branches which mark the

position of the end of the first season's growth. These will be developed to become the new leader and the first major branch. If these branches are not present you will still be able to detect the 'eyes' or locations of the dormant buds from which such branches will grow. The initial cut should be made in precisely the same way as illustrated, and within a few weeks the new shoots will emerge. This operation should be carried out in early spring, before the buds have opened. This process of allowing extension growth and pruning back to suitably positioned shoots or nodes should be repeated another two to four times – no more – before the final height is attained. A tree with too many sharp bends in a tall trunk looks unnatural.

2 The branch on the left is chosen to become the new leader and is pruned at the point where the next angle is planned, just above a pair of buds.

3 Select a large clay pot to encourage rapid growth and development. The long roots should be shortened to promote a compact root structure. Water and feed well.

4 Plant the tree at an angle so that one branch is horizontal, and the other – the new leader – points upwards, but in the opposite direction.

5 After a few weeks of vigorous growth, encouraged by heavy feeding, a mass of new shoots will have appeared. The first cycle is complete and it is time for more pruning.

7 Two shoots are left to become the second branch and the new leader. This time another shoot is also left at the rear to form the first back branch.

8 Another few weeks pass and the maple is ready for its third prune of the season. Free draining soil with frequent watering and feeding produces this vigorous growth, essential for rapid trunk development.

6 Maples produce a lot of small shoots around pruning scars. These should be thinned out so all the tree's energy is concentrated in the developing trunk.

9 The third pruning leaves three side branches, one to the rear, and four sections of trunk. One more year and the structure will be complete.

1 Before you start, make sure the plant is in good health and is firmly tied into its container. This will help prevent too much strain on the roots during cutting. The best time for this technique is early spring, before the production of new foliage has used up any of the tree's stored energy.

2 Decide how tall you want the trunk to be – the ideal proportion is about four times its width. Using a very sharp, fine-toothed saw, make two cuts which form an unequal 'V'-shaped surface.

Broom style zelkova

There is only one species which is eminently suitable for this style – the Japanese grey-barked elm, zelkova serrata, and it is no coincidence that it grows in this habit in nature. Other deciduous species can be used, but none perform as well. The creation of such a geometric, uniform branch structure requires an equally precise and calculated approach, which is almost invariably successful. The only element of chance is in the placement of the new shoots as they emerge from the severed trunk. However, there are normally so many that you would be very unlucky not to get off to a good start with a few of them. The plant you select must have a trunk thickness anything from three-quarters of an inch to four inches or more. If the trunk is too thin it will be impossible to execute the initial cut accurately and it is more likely to throw out shoots from lower down rather than from the cambium layer exposed by the cut. Once the sequence illustrated has been followed, adopt an annual regime of allowing shoots to grow four or five leaves and then trimming back to two. A vigorous, well fed tree may require this treatment several times during each growing season. Prune out crossing branches in late winter. Gradually you will build up a network of evenly spaced branches with ever-decreasing internodes.

3 Clean up any ragged edges with a sharp knife and seal the entire cut surface, especially around the edge, where the cambium layer is located.

4 Within six or seven weeks new shoots should push through the sealant. Sometimes these shoots take longer to appear, so be patient.

5 Tie some waterproof tape tightly around the emerging shoots. This ensures a smooth transition from trunk to branch without unsightly swelling.

6 The new shoots will grow rapidly. By the time they have reached this size they will have hardened off and will be ready for a prune.

7 The long shoots are all cut back to two or three leaves. You may need to thin out some of the weaker shoots as well.

8 New shoots will grow from each leaf axil, and they, too, will be shortened. This cycle will need to be repeated many times over.

▲ A classic broom style is shown here. It would have taken up to ten years or more to develop this fine tracery of twigs.

1 To create a jin, cut through the bark around the base of the branch. Then make another cut along its length. Make the cut 'eye-shaped' as marked in white.

2 Squeezing the bark with some flat-jawed pliers helps separate the bark from the wood. This is especially effective during spring and summer, when the sap is on the move.

Jins

One interpretation of the Japanese term jin is 'Godhead', but its definition in bonsai terms is rather less spiritual. Basically a jin is a dead branch which has shed its bark. In nature such branches are etched by the wind and rain and become bleached by the sun. They are frequently seen on most old conifers and even on some deciduous trees, notably oak. By artificially creating jins on a bonsai you can impart a feeling of great age, and when done with care, their form and colour can complement the foliage masses to great effect. Get into the habit of creating jins every time you branch prune conifers, rather than removing the branch completely. If you don't like it after having lived with it for a while you can always cut it off

3 The bark should peel away quite easily. If you are doing this in the autumn you may find the bark is a bit more stubborn, and you may need to scrape the wood clean.

4 A natural-looking shape and texture can be repeated by peeling back slivers of wood, exposing the grain. Jins look better if they are randomly formed rather than being carved.

▼ By creating jins out of selected branches we have increased the apparent age of this juniper.

later. You can create jins at normal pruning time, but the best time is during the summer, when the bark is full of sap and is easier to strip and the wound will heal quickly. Once you have made the jin you can give it texture by tearing the grain or by carving and sanding it to the desired shape. A jin will appear larger with a coarse texture than it would if given a smoother finish, so remember: the smaller the bonsai, the smoother the jin. Another good point to bear in mind is that on a developing bonsai the foliage masses will grow, but the jins won't! If your new jins look too big now, they may well be in better proportion in a few year's time, so don't be too hasty in reducing their size first.

5 The shaped jin can be refined, and any fuzz can be removed, with fine sandpaper, or a piece of broken glass, although don't sand the jin perfectly smooth.

6 In nature jins are bleached by the sun. In bonsai this effect is achieved by treating them with lime sulphur, which also preserves the wood. Lime sulphur smells foul, so work outside.

Sharis

1 Mark the outline of the shari with white paint before you cut. Make the line of the shari echo the shape of the trunk. Cut through to the wood.

Sharis are related to jins but reflect a much more dramatic struggle with nature, causing a loss of bark from the trunk. This could be the result of lightning, disease, the battle with the elements, or it may just be the way the tree naturally ages. Like jins, sharis are more appropriate on conifer bonsai, but for inspiration on deciduous trees take a look at our lowland pollarded willows with split trunks, or ancient hollow oaks.

The extreme use of sharis is employed in the creation of driftwood style bonsai. They are carved and refined to form wonderful shapes and textures which become more visually significant than the foliage masses. This is true living sculpture which, with the right balance of driftwood, tree and pot, represents the highest level of bonsai as an art form.

It is best to take several seasons to create an extensive shari, stripping of a little more bark each time. Bark is part of the tree's transport system, so always leave enough to support the foliage. On no account remove bark from immediately below a branch or it will die. Never allow a shari to encircle the trunk completely or the tree will die above that point.

Junipers will live happily with a spiral of living bark provided the sharis is created gradually over several seasons.

2 If you do this in summer, when the sap is flowing, the bark will come away cleanly. The dark area is where the exposed wood of the original shari has weathered.

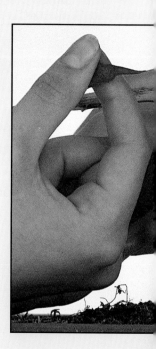

3 Seal the edges of the shari with narrow strips of cut paste in order to prevent the cut surfaces from drying out.

4 Note how the shari and jins flow from one another. Also, note how the shari runs from one side of the trunk to the other, enhancing the natural movement of the trunk line.

Pines will accept a gentle curve but spruces require a more or less straight line of living tissue from root to branch. Give the bonsai the proper aftercare by placing it in a lightly sheltered spot until all the remaining branches show new growth.

Lime sulphur does preserve the exposed wood as well as bleaching it, but one application lasts for only a short time. However, its effect is cumulative so repeated twice-yearly applications will eventually almost 'fossilise' the wood. Very large areas of exposed wood may begin to decay at the base, where the trunk is constantly moist. These areas can be treated with clear horticultural preservative, a little at a time. But don't let any run off into the soil.

5 As with jins, the exposed wood must be treated with lime sulphur to preserve and bleach it. The old shari will blend with the new one after a couple of applications.

Refining the image

When fully refined and preened, ready for display, the bonsai image should appear almost as if it is frozen in time. Each branch should be perfectly positioned and clearly defined, with each neatly trimmed foliage pad floating in its own space. As with all artistic disciplines, much depends on the aesthetic taste of the individual, but it is surprising how many experienced bonsai artists always seem to return to the classic Japanese principles, which have, after all, been developed over many years. There is a grace and poise about classic Japanese bonsai, which can literally take your breath away. The ability to create a near-perfect image by using the minimum number of elements has taken many centuries to develop and refine, and will continue to set the standard for many years to come. No bonsai is perfect, and the fact that all bonsai are living, growing plants means that they are constantly changing, and therefore require repeated attention to maintain their image. Even so, they can only look their absolute best for a few weeks at a time, after which they will, again, gradually begin to outgrow their ideal form. This tree has had its image refined for the first time, but there are still many faults in the design. Over the next five or six years it will go through similar processes many more times, hopefully improving on each occasion. Eventually it may reach the stage where I am totally satisfied with it. In a way I hope this never happens, because then the challenge will end. At some point in the distant future, a new owner may decide to change the front, or the planting angle. Perhaps the whole style may even be changed and by removing and reshaping branches, or lowering the apex. The comments and diagrams on these pages form a kind of critical analysis of the existing design, and offer some suggestions for alternative styles. Hopefully, these will help to guide your thoughts during those quiet moments of contemplation, when you and your tree plan your futures together.

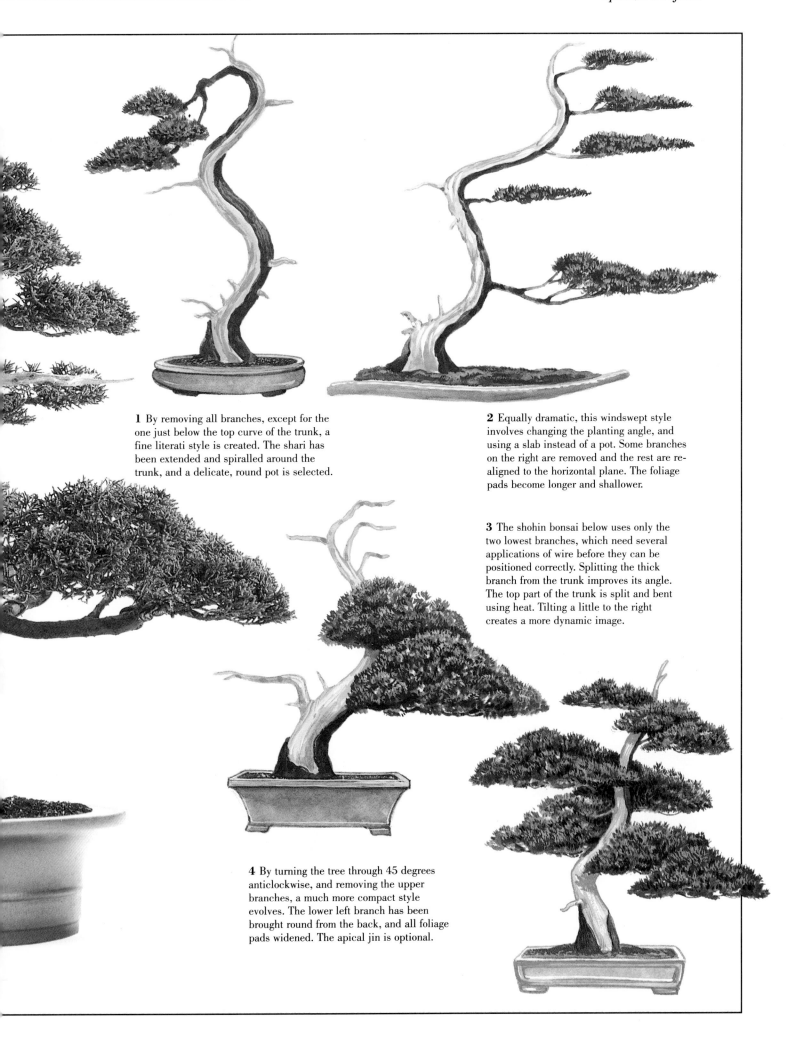

1 By removing all branches, except for the one just below the top curve of the trunk, a fine literati style is created. The shari has been extended and spiralled around the trunk, and a delicate, round pot is selected.

2 Equally dramatic, this windswept style involves changing the planting angle, and using a slab instead of a pot. Some branches on the right are removed and the rest are re-aligned to the horizontal plane. The foliage pads become longer and shallower.

3 The shohin bonsai below uses only the two lowest branches, which need several applications of wire before they can be positioned correctly. Splitting the thick branch from the trunk improves its angle. The top part of the trunk is split and bent using heat. Tilting a little to the right creates a more dynamic image.

4 By turning the tree through 45 degrees anticlockwise, and removing the upper branches, a much more compact style evolves. The lower left branch has been brought round from the back, and all foliage pads widened. The apical jin is optional.

Care

As with all plants the care and maintainence of trees and shrubs is important. With bonsai this factor is paramount. The small size of the plant, its roots and leaves means that extra attention is required.

Tools and wire

All you really need in the way
of equipment for your first
attempts at growing bonsai are
those which you probably
already have.
A pair of sharp scissors
Wire cutters
Secateurs (the bypass type,
not the anvil variety)
Nail scissors for fine work
A pointed steel hook for
combing out roots.
These tools will do the job as
well as any specialist
Japanese tools shown. But as
you gain in experience you
will begin to find these tools a
little clumsy at best and
totally inadequate at worst.
Sooner or later it will become
a necessity to invest in proper
bonsai tools, but rather than
spend a lot of money on a full
set buy each tool as you feel
you need it.

Here we show a variety of
types and thicknesses of
wire. Your first choice may be
influenced by economy and
availability. Copper wire can
be stripped from offcuts of
electrical cable, and green,
plastic-covered steel wire is
readily available at garden
centres. However, once you
have tried the custom-made
product you will never want to
use anything else. The wide
variety of gauges, make them
a joy to work with.

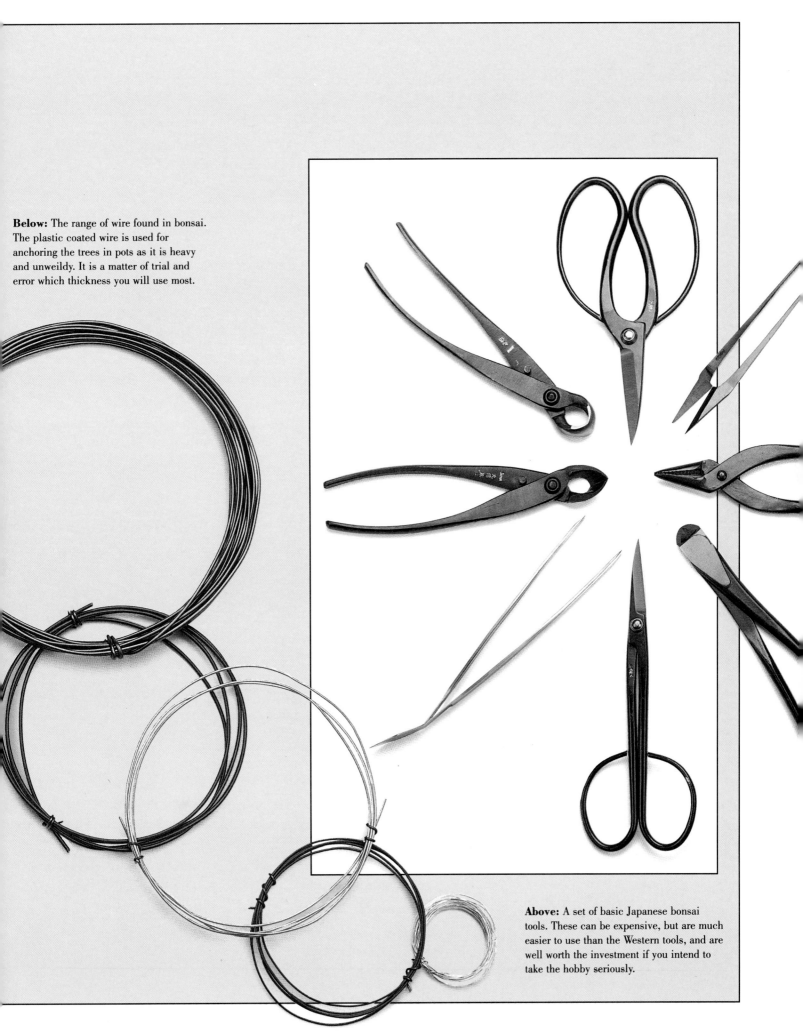

Below: The range of wire found in bonsai. The plastic coated wire is used for anchoring the trees in pots as it is heavy and unweildy. It is a matter of trial and error which thickness you will use most.

Above: A set of basic Japanese bonsai tools. These can be expensive, but are much easier to use than the Western tools, and are well worth the investment if you intend to take the hobby seriously.

Soils

Most plants will survive for limited periods in almost any growing medium – clay, sand, even pure water – but in order to thrive they need rather more. Since bonsai are grown in shallow containers for many years their requirements are quite specific. But before we discuss soil recipes let's consider the various functions of soil. The soil's most obvious function is to retain enough moisture and nutrients to ensure a steady supply to the roots between waterings. The soil must protect the roots from decay by allowing the free drainage of excess water. It must also contain air spaces so the roots can breathe. Finally, the soil anchors the tree in its pot, so it should not be too light.

Soil recipes

The standard bonsai soil recipe, which has been tried and tested for many years, contains just two ingredients which, when sifted and mixed in roughly equal proportions, satisfy these four basic requirements.

Organic matter

Organic matter satisfies the first of the four requirements mentioned above. This can be moss peat (as opposed to sedge peat), well-rotted leaf mould, composted forest bark or any of the peat substitutes which are becoming increasingly common. Don't use any farmyard manure or garden compost, however well rotted, as you will risk introducing all manner of soil-born diseases. If you collect your own leaf mould remove any unrotted material which will use up nitrogen from the fertiliser as it decays.

Grit

Grit, or sifted sharp sand, keeps the soil structure open and adds weight, thus satisfying the remaining three requirements. It can be quite difficult to find suitable grit, and many people resort to buying horticultural sharp sand and sifting out unsuitably-sized particles. This is extremely laborious, time consuming and wasteful – only about twenty percent of the original volume is useful. Builders sharp sand should never be used as it often contains impurities which can be harmful to plants. Flint grit, as used for alpine composts, is good but it has sharp edges which can damage the roots if used carelessly. So be gentle when repotting and don't use too much pressure. By far the best type I have tried is granite grit.

Additives

An increasing number of soil conditioners are available to the amateur gardener, ranging from volcanic lava to calcined (baked) clay. The main advantage of using such additives is that they perform the same functions as both organic matter and grit. That is to say they drain well but also retain moisture. Some growers use calcined clay instead of organic matter, and others find trees grown in pure lava do exceptionally well. It is always worth experimenting.

NOTE: all soil ingredients must be well sifted to remove all the coarse lumps and, more importantly, all the fine particles. Ideally you should be left with particles ranging in size between 2 and 4mm. Any particles finer than this may be difficult to wet once they dry out.

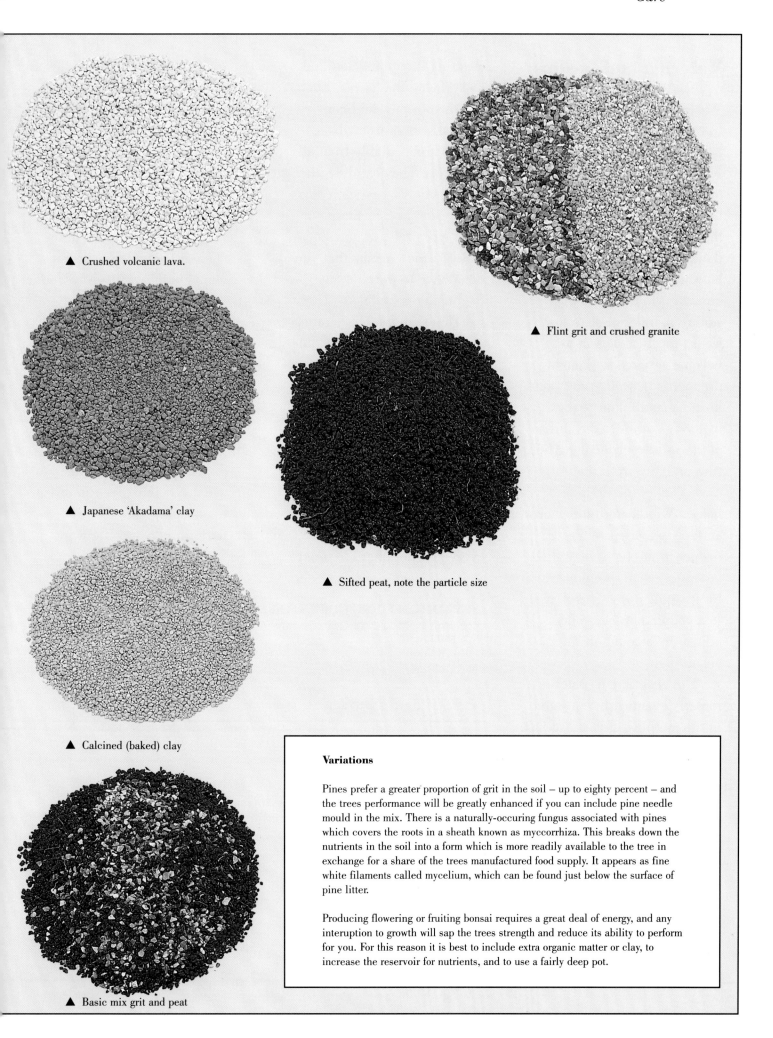

▲ Crushed volcanic lava.

▲ Flint grit and crushed granite

▲ Japanese 'Akadama' clay

▲ Sifted peat, note the particle size

▲ Calcined (baked) clay

Variations

Pines prefer a greater proportion of grit in the soil – up to eighty percent – and the trees performance will be greatly enhanced if you can include pine needle mould in the mix. There is a naturally-occuring fungus associated with pines which covers the roots in a sheath known as myccorrhiza. This breaks down the nutrients in the soil into a form which is more readily available to the tree in exchange for a share of the trees manufactured food supply. It appears as fine white filaments called mycelium, which can be found just below the surface of pine litter.

Producing flowering or fruiting bonsai requires a great deal of energy, and any interuption to growth will sap the trees strength and reduce its ability to perform for you. For this reason it is best to include extra organic matter or clay, to increase the reservoir for nutrients, and to use a fairly deep pot.

▲ Basic mix grit and peat

Watering and feeding

Watering

In theory, provided your bonsai is in a free-draining soil, it should not be possible to over water. But many beginners, manage to do just that. Over watering eliminates the air contained in the spaces between the soil particles and 'drowns' the roots. Having said this, it does take a few weeks for the problem to become serious, so the odd drenching now and then won't hurt. Generally the best method is to water the surface of the soil evenly, using a fine rose or spray, until the water drains out of the drainage holes. Wind can dry the soil's surface to a crisp, while deeper in the pot it may still be quite wet. If in doubt check by scraping away the surface in a couple of places and adjust the amount of water accordingly.

The best time to water is in early evening. If you water in the morning the tree doesn't have much of a chance to refresh itself before the heat of the day. All bonsai appreciate a daily shower.

Feeding

This can be a source of much confusion for the novice but the principle is really quite simple. There are three ways to apply fertiliser: by placing pellets on or in the soil, by watering it onto the soil and by spraying the leaves. Each has its own pros and cons. Specialist bonsai fertiliser pellets are available from all nurseries. They can be either the organic variety such as rape seed cake, or inorganic. Both types release nutrients slowly, which means that you don't have to worry about feeding for a while.

There are a large number of soluble fertilisers available in garden centres and florists, most of which are suitable. These can be routinely applied once a week or, better still, at a quarter strength with every watering. Never use a stronger solution than the manufacturers state. It is a good idea to change brand every now and then, in order to maintain a balanced diet. In prolonged spells of very wet weather you may not be able to feed your trees since they may not need any water. Research has shown that a plant can absorb more nutrients through its leaves than through its roots. Many standard soluble fertilisers can be applied this way. Foliar feeds are easily to apply provided you don't do so in strong sun, otherwise the leaves may scorch.

Any of these methods of feeding are suitable for keeping an established tree in good health and vigour, but occasionally you may need to use a specialist feed in order to encourage the tree to perform in a specific way.

SEASONAL FEEDING GUIDES FOR ESTABLISHED BONSAI

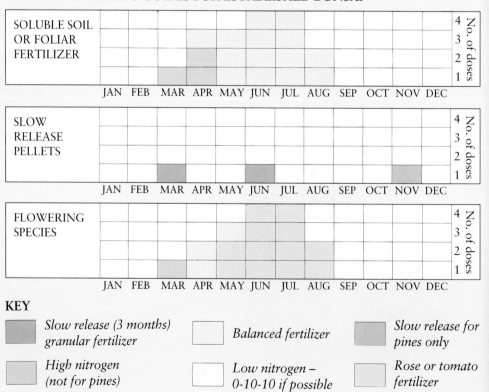

needs it, not before. So in spring, after growth has started, or once new leaves have emerged following leaf pruning, an application of a high nitrogen feed will replenish the tree's resources.

Phosphorus (P) is especially useful after repotting or when a tree is recovering from a root problem, so a little extra can be given at such times. A pinch of powdered superphosphorate on the surface of the soil is an easy method of application.

NPK?

These letters appear on the packs of all good fertilisers. The letters are the chemical symbols for the three major nutrients and the numbers denote their ratio. But what do each of the elements do?

Nitrogen

This is responsible for leaf and stem growth and can enrich the colour of the foliage.

Phosphorus

This is primarily responsible for root growth. It also encourages thick, sturdy trunks.

Potassium

Potassium, or potash, is responsible for encouraging flowers and fruit as well as hardening off late growth before the winter.

Special feeding

Here are some pointers as to why this should be done.

Nitrogen (N) should be increased when you want a plant to put on a spurt of rapid growth. A high nitrogen feed should be applied as the tree

Potassium (K) should be increased for all flowering and fruiting bonsai. Potash can also be increased to help weak plants regain strength. A little sulphate of potash sprinkled on the soil once a week will do the trick.

Preparing for a display

When bonsai are in a public show they come under very close scrutiny. It is essential that when your works of art are displayed they look their best. They should be sparkling with health and spotlessly clean. All debris such as dead or discoloured leaves must be removed, and the surface of the soil must be free of weeds. The trunk and main branches will probably need cleaning, as will the pot. It is very attempting to use bamboo or split can as a backdrop to a display, but this is far too 'busy' and detracts attention from the trees. It is far better to use a pale, neutral coloured, untextured surface. The same goes for the table, although woven reed matting can be used provided the trees are displayed on simple, low wooden stands. If you don't have suitable stands you can construct some low boxes and paint them the same colour as the backdrop. The important thing is to keep it simple. Keep labels small and information basic. You only need to state the species (botanical and common names), the style and the age. The owner's or artist's name can also be included. Also, remember that the public will love to touch your bonsai, so take whatever precautions you can to prevent this happening. It is not unknown for people to try to take cuttings from bonsai displays!

▲ The finished display.

1 Study the outline of the tree carefully and snip off anything which breaks the style. A photograph often reveals faults the eye misses.

2 Pick out all weeds and dead moss, making sure to pull out all the roots as well. This is good general practice anyway, even if you are not exhibiting the tree.

3 You can make the surfa by dressing it with fresh s with extra grit looks good, alone is too clean and loo

4 Juniper trunks should have all the flaky bark brushed off with an old toothbrush. Stubborn bits of bark in awkward places can be rubbed off with sandpaper.

5 Once the bark has been removed, the trunk can be given added colour by burnishing it with a soft, lint-free cloth, moistened with just a little vegetable oil.

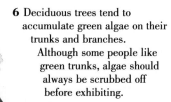

6 Deciduous trees tend to accumulate green algae on their trunks and branches. Although some people like green trunks, algae should always be scrubbed off before exhibiting.

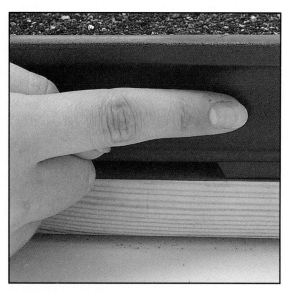

7 Glazed pots just need to be washed, but unglazed pots need to be rubbed down with wire wool or fine sandpaper to remove all the blemishes and lime scale.

8 Additional patina can be given to unglazed pots by rubbing the surface with a very slightly oily finger. Too much oil will make the surface too shiny and will ruin the effect.

ctive
soil
t
e.

Siting your bonsai

The choice of site for your bonsai display will depend largely on the layout of your garden, but it is important to consider your bonsai's requirements as well. Although different species prefer different conditions, it will help if you can keep all your collection in the same part of the garden in order to make daily watering and inspection a lot easier Conifers generally love to be in full sun all day and can even tolerate the heating of the pot and soil. Some tough deciduous species, such as elm, birch and hawthorn, also enjoy the sun but prefer their roots to be kept cooler. This can be achieved by placing them so that their pots are shaded from the afternoon sun by other trees. Species with more delicate foliage, like Japanese maples, hornbeam and beech, need to be protected from strong winds as well as sun. Azaleas also suffer from over-exposure to wind and sun. However, this does not mean that they should be placed in total shade. Morning and evening sun can do no harm, but during the middle of the day they should be in the shadow of a nearby building or full-grown tree. Failing this, you can construct a canopy of greenhouse shading mesh which will simulate the dappled shade of the woodland margin where these plants naturally thrive.

Bonsai growing in small pots will all need a certain amount of shade, regardless of the species. Small pots heat up quickly, cooking the roots and drying the soil. A permanent area of shade featuring a slatted roof eliminating fifty percent of the sunlight is ideal. If you can't arrange this then put your trees against a

1 Wooden trellis is not effective as a backdrop, but does provide dappled shade. The smaller trees are protected from the strong sun by the larger ones.

2 Displays which are open to the public need to be protected from curious visitors by a discreet rail. Paving slabs set in coarse gravel guide the viewer along the display. Two trees are temporarily placed on the gravel, in the shade of a cedar tree, while they recover from reporting.

west-facing wall, but remember to turn them round at regular intervals otherwise the branches at the rear will slow down and may eventually die. Keep all bonsai on tables or custom-built benches – never on the ground. Every pest known to the gardener: slugs, ants, cats and even kids will conspire to destroy your collection in no time. Besides this, when your trees are displayed at eye-level you can appreciate them much more and will be able to spot pests and diseases a lot sooner. Benches could have slatted surfaces to allow air to circulate around the trees and the water to drain away. Leave plenty of space between the trees so the lower branches receive light and air. Move them around occasionally so each side of the trees receive their fair share of sun. Large bonsai can be stood on 'monkey poles' – stout wooden posts with a platform firmly fixed to the top.

If you decide to go the whole way and construct a Japanese-style bonsai garden, keep it simple. Avoid the temptation to include too many lanterns, pagodas, stone buddha's and other Oriental 'garden gnomes'. The inclusion of some low-growing, lush plants like hostas and dwarf bamboo can help retain local humidity which will benefit the bonsai.

3 The insulated polycarbonate wall of a greenhouse makes an ideal backdrop for bonsai, as this one at Heron's Nursery. Note how the suiseki (viewing stones) add interest.

Winter protection

Most fully hardy species tolerate having their pots frozen solid for short periods at a time. Pines and spruces even seem to thrive on this treatment, preferring it to any form of protection at all, other than a temporary wind break. But the ravages of winter can take their toll on most other species in a number of ways. Constant freezing and thawing of the pot every day can devastate a root system, especially if the pot never entirely thaws before re-freezing. Remember a waterlogged soil expands more on freezing than a comfortably moist one. Trident maples and Chinese elms have thick, fleshy roots which are particularly at risk. Even large bonsai of these species should be placed in winter

1 Good hygiene is essential. Pick off dead leaves, which harbour pests and diseases over winter. At the same time, pick off any scale insects you find.

2 It is a good idea to peel away surface moss, which can harbour insect pests and fungal spores. This is essential on small bonsai which are going to be buried in peat.

confinement. Although roots are inactive most of the time during winter, moisture is still lost through the bark. Under normal circumstances the tree would contain enough reserves and the roots could replenish the supply during mild weather. Expanding buds also demand a supply of moisture which frozen roots cannot provide. Sunny days can induce both transpiration and bud activity, but may not succeed in thawing the roots as well. Wind and sun can cause pots to dry out even in winter. Although this may not affect the tree directly it will kill the finer roots, putting the whole system at risk of decay and more vulnerable to damage by wet, freezing conditions. Saturated soil not only increases the risk of frost damage, it also creates the ideal environment for root rot.

PROTECTIVE MEASURES
A few simple precautions can guarantee a long and happy

life to your bonsai. Although the worst of the weather comes after Christmas in the northern hemisphere, it is as well to have the protection complete by the end of November. Early change will only be compounded later. There are five basic ways to site your bonsai over winter, each offering them a different degree of protection.

Wind protection
Pots are stood on bricks or boxes between the benches. If the benches run east/west, place a board at the eastern end to prevent a wind-tunnel effect.

Shelter
A covered area, closed on three sides and open on the fourth, preferably western side. The easiest solution is to place the trees on bricks under the benches. Cover the benches with clear polythene and weight it down securely on three sides.

3 Small bonsai should be gently teased from their pots and plunged in a box of loose peat. Cover the root mass with a one-inch layer of loose peat to insulate.

Winter confinement

This involves protecting the tree against wind, sun, rain and rapid temperature change. It doesn't offer a totally frost-free environment as this would disturb dormancy in hardy trees. Deciduous trees can be kept in a shed – they need no light until spring.

Frost-free

If you are not sure about the hardiness of an unusual species then it is as well to keep it in a cool conservatory or unheated room through the winter.

What kind of protection

The table provides a basic guide. By early spring you can begin to re-introduce your bonsai to their benches, tucking the smaller ones up at night during exceptionally cold weather.

4 An ideal impromptu bonsai shelter. A considerable number of trees can be packed in the spaces below the benches, and the whole thing covered in heavy duty polythene. During spells of really severe weather the front of this shelter can be rolled down to give the bonsai extra protection.

GUIDE TO WINTER PROTECTION

Large bonsai
Pines and spruces – open
Junipers – open, give blue-leaved varieties wind protection.
Very hardy species (English elm, field maple, larch, birch, hawthorn, yew etc.) – wind protection. Shelter from prolonged rain.
Hardy species – (Japanese maples, ornamentals) – shelter.
Temperamental plants (red maples, spring flowering varieties) – shelter.
Trident maples and Chinese elm – winter confinement.

Medium size bonsai
Pines and spruces – open, wind protection in very severe weather.
Junipers, very hardy species – wind protection, shelter in harsh weather.
Hardy species – shelter.
Temperamental plants, tridents and Chinese elms – winter confinement.

Small bonsai
Pines and spruces – wind protection, very small bonsai need shelter.
Junipers, very hardy and hardy species – winter confinement. Remove smaller trees from their pots and bury them in boxes of damp peat.
Temperamental plants, tridents and Chinese elms – Winter confinement, small trees packed in peat boxes. In extreme cold place trees where the temperature remains just above freezing. An unheated room may be too warm. A thermostatically-controlled heater for your shed is ideal.

1 Aphids, surely the most common of all pests, here shown in juvenile and adult stage on pine. There are many distinct species, but all succumb readily to conventional garden pesticides.

2 Adelgids form a waxy residue on pine shoots, and can kill them. Detergent in the solution helps penetrate the waxy protection.

3 Scale insects come in many different sizes. These, on a Chinese juniper, are tiny and difficult to spot with the naked eye. Tiny specs of white invite closer inspection.

4 These scale insects are easier to spot once mature. The big ones can be picked off, the smaller ones killed with systemic insecticide. A 'winter-wash' gets rid of overwintering eggs.

Pests and diseases

Bonsai are prone to the same diseases and pests that attack full size trees, but because they are small and compact, it doesn't take long at all for a localised problem to spread over the entire tree, with disastrous results. And because it grows slowly a bonsai is less able to outgrow an infection, or a plague of aphids, in the same way a full-size tree can. A twice-yearly precautionary treatment with a systemic insecticide and fungicide will help, but it will not be one hundred percent successful. (Systemic chemicals are designed to be absorbed by the plant and fight the problem from the inside.) Deciduous trees will benefit from a normal garden 'winter wash'. Constant vigilance is necessary throughout the year. Once a problem has been spotted and diagnosed remedial action should be taken immediately, using an appropriate commercial treatment.

Always read the pack to make sure the treatment is effective for your particular problem, and follow the manufacturer's instructions to the letter. If one brand doesn't appear to work try another – some insects seem to be able to build up a tolerance if the same brand is used all the time.

Trees may take weeks to recover from fungal infections, so don't lose heart. If the symptoms stop getting worse, the treatment has more than likely worked. Never use systemic on Chinese elms. They will not kill the tree but the foliage will yellow and fall and fine twigs may die back.

7 These trans caused by the which burrow the surface of unsightly but affected folia

6 The adult vine weevil is not a pest in itself, but it can lay eggs at any time of year. These rapidly hatch, producing the voracious little grub illustrated above. Squash on sight!

5 This ugly little beast is the scourge of all bonsai buffs. It is the notorious vine weevil which can devour a pot full of roots in no time. Treat soil with Gamma HCH and check soil when repotting.

are
ub,
below

move

8 Many trees are attacked by tiny mites which stimulate galls to form on the leaves, like these on elm. Removing all infected leaves in June is the only known cure.

9 Papery brown patches like these are most likely caused by too-strong insecticide, or the sun shining through water water droplets, which act like magnifying glasses.

10 Caterpillars are quite harmless in small numbers. Loners, like this comma butterfly, can be left alone, but remove colonies by hand.

11 'Pine needle cast' starts as yellowing blotches on the needles, which soon fall. This seriously damages full-size trees and can kill bonsai, especially weak or newly collected trees. Once diagnosed, treat monthly with Bordeaux mixture or 'Zineb' until September.

12 Red spider mites are microscopic sap-sucking creatures which infest plants in vast numbers, even in mid-winter. The leaves or needles turn brown in patches, and sometimes a minute web can be detected.

13 Poor air circulation is mainly responsible for powdery mildew, which can easily kill young shoots. Cure with appropriate garden fungicide but prevention is better.

Spring

EARLY SPRING

Repotting
Any healthy deciduous trees you have not been able to repot yet should be attended to in the first part of this month. You can keep deciduous trees in an outhouse if necessary at this time. However, as soon as the buds begin to burst you must place the tree outside.

Pruning
Deciduous trees can be pruned once the buds begin to show signs of activity.

Wiring
Start wiring deciduous trees – fine twigs as well as thick branches – before the buds swell if possible. If the buds have already started to move take extra care as they are easily dislodged at this crucial stage in their development.

Watering
Keep soil just moist. Be especially careful not to allow newly-repotted trees to become too wet.

Feeding
Do not feed newly repotted trees until the buds are open.

General
Inspect the soil surface of trees which are not being repotted this year.

MID-SPRING
Now things are really hotting up. Buds are bursting and roots are growing rapidly.

Repotting
If you haven't finished repotting deciduous trees it is best to leave them for next year unless they are really rootbound.

Pruning
Prune back hard.

Wiring
Wire spruce, juniper and pine but not deciduous trees.

Watering
Now your watering routine will get under way.

Feeding
Don't fertilise newly repotted trees. Those repotted last month can be given their first spring feed if growth has started.

LATE SPRING

Repotting
All repotting should be finished by the first week.

Pruning
Trees in training can be pruned now.

Wiring
Conifers can now be wired, but take care not to damage the new growth.

Trimming
Pinch expanding pine candles as they grow. Start with the small ones and finish with the larger ones a week or so later.

Watering
Now the trees are in full swing they will need watering at least once a day.

Feeding
Late developers can be given a little extra nitrogen, others should now be receiving a balanced diet on a regular basis.

Summer

EARLY SUMMER

Repotting
Only Chinese junipers can be repotted with confidence now provided they are kept sheltered from drying winds and full sun for a while.

Pruning
Start to prune pines and spruce now. Begin with the smaller branches and do the larger ones later in the month.

Wiring
Wire away to your hearts content on anything that takes your fancy.

Feeding
Continue with a regular balanced feed.

MID-SUMMER
Your trees will have slowed down by now, resting before their second surge of growth later in the month.

Pruning
Wounds will heal quickly at this time of year.

Trimming
Carry on as last month where necessary.

Wiring
Wire away, especially conifers.

Watering
Carry on as last month, only more so. It is by now especially important to water in the early evening if possible.

Feeding
As last month. Give high potash feeds to bonsai.

General
Continue everyday health checks and inspect wire at the same time.

LATE SUMMER
Older foliage can begin to look a bit tired this month, although many trees will still be growing rapidly.

Pruning
Wounds heal quickly if pruning is carried out by the middle of the month.

Trimming
This is less necessary now, with the exception of junipers.

Wiring
Wire applied now to deciduous species is unlikely to have much affect until growth starts next year.

Watering
This is just as hectic as last month. Make sure that pots which become very dry are thoroughly soaked.

Feeding
Reduce nitrogen this month, eliminating it completely during the last week.

General
Remove weeds, dying leaves and adventitious shoots, and keep up the pest control.

Autumn

EARLY AUTUMN

Trimming
Not necessary now – except for those persistent junipers, which will carry on growing for another month or so.

Watering
As your trees begin to slow down so can you. Be vigilant, though, changeable weather can deceive you, and pots can still dry out surprisingly quickly.

Feeding
Nitrogen-free fertiliser all month. Additional bonemeal applied to pines, whose roots remain slightly active all winter, will be appreciated by them early next year.

MID-AUTUMN

Wiring
Remove tight wire by carefully cutting it away from the branches. Don't attempt to re-apply if it involves additional bending of the branch until next spring.

Watering
Only when necessary. For the next two months pots can still dry out but mists and dew may make the surface appear wet, while the soil below may be quite dry.

LATE AUTUMN
The last leaves of autumn fall, to reveal the fine tracery twigs your summer-long trimming has produced. Rich, green conifers sparkle with frost. A time to contemplate your bonsai with satisfaction, and appreciate the fruits of your labour.

Repotting
Raw material can be dug up and potted into large containers or growing beds, if the species is fully hardy.

Pruning
Only rough pruning of raw material is necessary. Even well-sealed wounds may die back around the edges over winter if the weather is severe enough.

Wiring
It is tempting to work on your trees when the branches are clear and the structure can be seen. But wiring now will encourage die-back, and lead to disappointment.

Watering
Only when necessary, but check every couple of days. Wind can dry pots almost as quickly as the sun.

Winter

EARLY WINTER
Nature shuts up shop and takes a well-earned rest – but you still have work to do.

Repotting
Finish potting up newly-collected raw material by the middle of the month, and protect the roots.

Pruning
Only rough pruning of raw material is safe now.

Wiring
Tempting, but resist.

Watering
Keep soil moist if the weather doesn't do it for you.

MID-WINTER
Trees stand motionless, tensed against the cold. The more time you spend with them now, the more you respect their endurance. There is little work for you to do.

Watering
Trees kept in the open will not need watering, in fact they may even need to be protected from excessive rain. A thick blanket of snow does no harm to large, hardy trees in the open.

LATE WINTER
Deep in the soil something begins to stir. The flower buds on quince and cherries begin to swell. Will this year's spring take a lie-in or will it rise early? A nail-biting time.

Repotting
Truly hardy deciduous trees can be repotted towards the end of the month if the roots are white at the tips. Protect them from hard frost and heavy rain until the buds start to open.

Pruning
You can begin to prune hardy deciduous trees if you are sure the remaining shoots and branches are in good health.

Wiring
Wire deciduous trees while the buds are still tight against the shoots. As the buds swell they become more fragile and are easily damaged and even more easily dislodged.

Watering
Keep repotted trees moist but not wet. Shelter them from constant rain.

Feeding
Trees which have already started to move, and conifers which did not receive their bonemeal last autumn, can be helped along with a dose of fish emulsion.

Glossary

This list contains botanical and horticultural terms relevant to bonsai as well as terms unique to bonsai.

ABSCISSON LAYER The layer of cork which forms at the base of the petiole on deciduous trees in autumn. This layer creates a seal preventing the flow of nutrients, causing the leaf to fall.

ACID Describes soils with a pH of less than 7.0. Although most trees will grow happily in acid soils, some, including field maple and beech, do better in alkaline conditions.

ADVENTITIOUS A term applied to shoots arising from parts of the plant other than the growing points, usually on older wood such as trunk or wound scars.

ALKALINE Describes soils with a pH of over 7.0, or rich in lime. Most trees will grow in alkaline soil, but others, notable azaleas, require acid conditions to survive. Alkalinity can be corrected by using any of the commercial soil acidifiers.

ALTERNATE Refers to leaves which appear singly, first on one side of the shoot, and then on the other.

APEX The tip of a shoot, or a tree, from which extension growth takes place. In bonsai this point is dictated by aesthetic considerations and is not necessarily the focus of the tree's energy.

APICAL Describes a shoot at the tip of a branch or a bud at the tip of a shoot.

AXIL, AXILLARY The angle between a leaf and its parent shoot, which always contains at least one bud. Also the angle between a vein and the midrib of a leaf.

BANKAN Bonsai style. A tree with a twisted or coiled trunk.

BARK A protective layer covering trunk and branches, consisting of living corky cells on the inside, generated annually by the cambium, and dead cells on the outside.

BASAL Applies to fresh growth arising from the base of a plant.

BLEEDING The excessive loss of sap from new wounds, often the plant's natural device to prevent infection entering the wound.

BLIND Describes a shoot which has failed to develop an apical bud.

BOLE The clear trunk of a tree, from ground level to the lowest branch.

BROADLEAVED Denotes any tree which is not a conifer.

BUD A tightly condensed embryonic shoot, usually protected by scales formed by modified leaves.

BUNJINGI Bonsai style (Literati). Originating in China during the T'ang dynasty, and reflecting calligraphic brush strokes.

BUTTRESS The swelling at the base of a trunk where the surface roots emerge.

CALCIFUGE A plant which cannot tolerate alkaline soil.

CALLUS The 'scar' tissue, generated by the cambium, which forms over a wound or at the base of a cutting prior to root initiation.

CAMBIUM The thin growing layer between the bark and the wood which is responsible for laying down new bark on the outside and new wood on the inside each growing season, increasing the girth of the trunk. The cambium layer also forms new roots on cuttings, new buds, and graft unions.

CANOPY The foliage-bearing upper and outer reaches of a tree.

CHLOROPHYLL The green substance in plants, whose function is to convert carbon dioxide from the air, and water from the soil, into carbohydrates, using sunlight as a catalyst (photosynthesis).

CHOKKAN Bonsai style (Formal upright). A straight, unbroken trunk, persisting to the tree's apex, with symmetrically arranged branches.

COLLAR The swelling at the point of union between a branch and the trunk.

COMPOST 1: Partially decayed vegetable matter. 2: A mixture of sand, humus and other ingredients used as a growing medium.

COMPOUND Describes a leaf which is made up of a number of leaflets, attached to a central rib.

CONIFER A cone-bearing tree, usually with needle-like leaves.

COTYLEDON The first leaves to emerge from a seed, usually thick and fleshy, and unlike the true leaves.

CROWN The upper part of a tree formed by the branches and upper trunk.

CUTICLE A waxy coating on a leaf which reduces moisture loss and helps to prevent damage by external factors such as frost.

CUTTING A section of stem, root or leaf which is taken for propagation.

DAMPING-OFF A fungal disease causing seedlings to collapse during the first few weeks after germination.

DECIDUOUS A tree or shrub which sheds its leaves each autumn.

DEFOLIATION Natural shedding or artificial removal of leaves.

DENDROLOGY The study of trees.

DIE-BACK The withering and death of shoots or branches due to disease, drought or some other adverse condition.

DORMANT 1: Describes a bud which did not produce growth during the season following its formation, but which retains the ability to produce growth in the future. 2: The resting period during autumn and winter when the tree puts on little or no growth.

DRAWN Refers to plants which have grown uncharacteristically tall and slender due to overcrowding or poor light.

DWARF A genetic mutation of a species producing a small, compact growth habit.

EPICORMIC Refers to growth emerging from dormant buds.

EVERGREEN A tree or shrub which bears foliage throughout the year.

EXOTIC A plant originating from another country, regardless of climate or location.

EYE An undeveloped bud on a shoot over one year old.

FERTILISER A substance which provides one or more essential plant nutrients.

FLUSH A surge of new growth. Most trees produce one flush in spring and another in mid-summer.

FORCING Accelerating the growth or development of a plant by artificially changing its growing conditions.

FUKINAGASHI Bonsai style (Windswept). Depicting a tree exposed to strong prevailing winds.

GALL An abnormal growth on a root, stem or leaf, caused by a microscopic insect.

GENUS A group of related species.

GIRTH The circumference of the trunk of a tree, measured at chest height in full size specimens.

GO-KAN Bonsai style – five trunked.

GRAFTING The vegetative bonding of one part of a plant to another.

HABIT The natural shape or growth pattern of a plant.

HABITAT The conditions and location in which a plant is normally found in nature.

HAN-KENGAI Bonsai style (Semi-cascade). The apex must fall below the rim of the pot but not below its base.

HALF-HARDY Describes a plant which can tolerate cold but not sub-zero temperatures.

HARDENING-OFF The process of gradually introducing a plant grown under protection to outside conditions.

HARDWOOD The term used for timber from broadleaved trees.

HARDY Describes a plant which can survive outside during winter.

HOKIDACHI Bonsai style (Broom). All branches emerge from the same point at the top of a short, straight trunk.

HUMUS Partially decayed organic matter present in the soil.

IKADABUKI Bonsai style (Raft). The plant is laid on its side and the branches are trained vertically to form many trunks.

INORGANIC Applies to any chemical compound which does not contain carbon.

INTERNODE The distance between the leaf nodes on a shoot

ISHITSUKI Bonsai style (Root on rock). A rock replaces the pot.

JIN A branch or trunk apex which has been stripped of its bark and preserved.

JOHN INNES A series of basic compost recipes containing sand, humus, loam and fertiliser.

JUVENILE Refers to foliage produced during stages of rapid growth which is distinct from adult foliage

KABUDACHI Bonsai style (clump). Several trunks arising from the same point on a root.

KENGAI Bonsai style (cascade). The apex is below the pot base.

KYONAL Proprietary Japanese wound sealant for bonsai

LATERAL A shoot emerging from a bud on a main stem.

LAYERING A means of propagating from mature growth by removing bark to encourage advantageous root growth to emerge form above the wound.

LEACHING The process by which nutrients and minerals are washed out of the soil by the passage of water.

LEADER The dominant shoot.

LENTICEL A pore on a shoot or stem of a tree.

LIME Calcium as a soil constituent.

LIME SULPHUR Originally used as an insecticide and fungicide, this compound is now used to preserve and bleach jins and sharis

LOOM Normal, good garden soil.

MAME Miniature bonsai, able to "sit comfortably in the palm of a hand".

MOYOGI Bonasi style (Informal upright). The trunk consists of a series of curves with symmetrically arranged branches.

NEAGARI Bonsai style (Exposed root).

NEBARI The exposed surface roots.

NETSUNANARI Bonsai style (Root connected). Several trunks arising from different points on the same root system.

NODE A stem joint or the point at which a leaf or leaves are attached to the stem.

ORGANIC Any chemical compound containing carbon.

pH a unit of measuring the acid/alkaline balance of a soil.

PHOTOSYNTHESIS The process by which a plant manufactures sugars by utilising light and chlorophyll to combine carbon dioxide and water.

SEKIJOJU Bonsai style (Root over rock).

SHAKAN Bonsai style (Slanting).

TAP ROOT The main downward growing root of a plant or young tree.

TENDER Describes a plant which cannot tolerate low temperatures.

TERMINAL Refers to the upper shoot, flower or bud.

TRANSPIRATION The continual passage of water vapour through pores on leaves and stems

VEGETATIVE Describes propagation by any means other than by seed.

Managing Editor: Jo Finnis
Editor: Sue Wilkinson
Design: Art of Design
Photography: Neil Sutherland
Production: Ruth Arthur; Sally Connolly; Neil Randles; Karen Staff; Matthew Dale; Jonathan Tickner
Production Director: Gerald Hughes

Acknowledgement: I am particularly grateful to my friends Peter Chan, of Heron's Nursery and Ruth Stafford-Jones, for allowing us to photograph trees from their private collections and Bill jordan for his advice and the loan of his photographs. Thanks also due to China Bonsai for the loan of their workshop.